Reunion

La Réunion

Finding Gilbert

Reunion
La Réunion

Finding Gilbert

Marshall & McClintic Publishing
200 Coyote Street #1122, Nevada City, CA 95959
MarshallMcClinticPublishing.com

This book is set in Adobe® Garamond Type Text.

Printed in the United States of America

First Edition: May 2014

ISBN-13: 978-0-9910446-0-3

To my father,
who taught me that love
is the most important thing

and to my husband, Landon,
for being the love of my life

Table of Contents

Table of Contents

They seem very ordinary
those moments that change
our lives forever

In reality, the moments just
before them were ordinary
and then everything stopped
or glowed or vibrated
and stood out
from the moment before

And looking back
it is clear
how life changed forever
in that instant

Prologue

October 1993
Normandy, France

Sunlight sparkled on the water of the English Channel, seagulls circled and dove and the rhythmic sound of the waves breaking in the distance floated up to where I stood at the top of the cliff.

With seven other American tourists, I had spent the day learning about the Normandy Invasion. Our French tour guide, Marcel, had shown us beaches with the code names of Sword, Juno, Gold, Utah—and now Omaha.

"See that beach down there?" Marcel pointed to the long expanse of sand below us that stretched out to sea.

"Peaceful, right?" We all nodded.

"Well, on June 6, 1944, that beach was anything but peaceful. You're looking down at the American landing beach that became known as "Bloody Omaha," for all the American soldiers who lost their lives there in the early hours of D-Day."

A seagull called. Waves sighed. Marcel turned to gesture at the fields behind us. "The cemetery behind you was designated as a piece of American soil in honor of the soldiers who were never able to return home."

We turned to look at the manicured green space, where almost ten thousand white crosses lined up in perfect symmetrical rows as far as we could see. Visitors whispered as they walked among the crosses, some searching for the name of a loved one. A baby's cry broke the stillness.

"Did you say that your father was in the D-Day invasion?" Marcel gestured to me.

"Yes, he was," I said. "In fact, he was one of those who landed on Omaha Beach. Now I know how lucky I was that he came back."

Marcel shook his head in agreement.

I'd never been interested in history. In school, I doodled and daydreamed during class, memorized dates for a test, then promptly forget them. I didn't see how what had happened in a bunch of wars in the past mattered in my life.

But two years before, my father had passed away. All my life, he'd told stories of his time in France during the war, and losing him made those memories more precious. I realized that I had a personal relationship to this historic event and with the 50th anniversary of the D-Day invasion coming up the following June 1994, found myself genuinely interested.

I'd begun to realize that my father's stories had influenced my life in ways that I was still discovering. And so I'd journeyed to France to learn all that I could.

The day had been moving and powerful. We visited small museums full of photos and memorabilia, uniforms and newspaper clippings. We watched footage of old newsreels, with Eisenhower speaking to shiny faced young men who were excited and eager to go into battle.

We learned that over five thousand ships, eleven thousand planes, eighteen thousand paratroopers and two hundred thousand soldiers had descended on the five landing beaches in the early hours of June 6th, 1944. The cost was high; more than 9,000 allied troops had been killed or wounded. We studied a giant relief map depicting the planes and ships, trying to understand the enormity of it all.

Our final stop of the day was the American Cemetery in Colleville-sur-Mer, situated on the cliff above Omaha Beach. Our guide gave us some time to walk around the impeccably manicured one hundred and seventy two acres. As I tried to digest all I'd seen and heard, I was grateful for the time alone.

I wandered into the small chapel on the grounds. On the ceiling, an artist had rendered an angel watching over a soldier and the inscription on the wall read, "Think not only upon their passing, remember the glory of their spirit."

I reflected on those words as I walked back to the cliffs again and sat down on a bench to try to sort out all my thoughts. Remembering my dad, the tears began to fall. I turned my face into the chilly fall wind off the sea and breathed in the fresh, salty air.

Dad's stories of the war had seemed like just that—stories, not completely real. But now I knew that he'd been a part of the largest land and sea invasion in the history of the world.

That made me wonder: after living so close to life-and-death, how had Dad and the other soldiers returned to a normal life? Nothing else would be as real as that ever again. So they must have been caught—between wanting to forget and not being able to.

No wonder there'd been a post-war baby boom, of which I was a part. After so much death and destruction, family life and babies must have seemed like a balm, a blessing.

I adored my father and thought I knew him well. But there was so much here he'd seen and experienced that he hadn't talked about. Why hadn't I encouraged him to come back to France again? Why hadn't I asked more questions and paid more attention, before it was too late?

As I looked out over the water, I remembered Dad's stories about the seven-year-old French orphan, Gilbert, who Dad had befriended during his five months in Normandy. Dad even tried to adopt the boy and bring him home.

In the months before my father died, when he talked about Gilbert, he'd seemed wistful. "I wonder what ever happened to him," he said.

Now, as I stood where Dad and Gilbert had become so close, I thought again about the little boy who could have become my older brother. Just as Dad's stories about the war gained substance from my being there, Gilbert, too, became more real. He was no longer just a character in one of Dad's stories.

Where would Gilbert be now? I wasn't even sure how to spell his last name. I just knew how it sounded—DesClos, Du-Clos? After fifty years, what chance would there be of tracking him down? And if I did somehow find him, would he even remember Dad? It all seemed impossible.

But maybe because I was where it had all happened, the idea began to haunt me. What if Gilbert was still out there somewhere, remembering my dad?

What if I could find him?

Part I
1944

1

My father, Donald Kenneth Johnson, a lieutenant junior grade in the 111th Battalion of the Seabees, the Civil Engineering Corps of the U.S. Naval Reserves, held a clipboard and looked out over the English Channel towards France.

A crisp wind off the water blew sand sideways and the sky threatened rain. He had just dismissed his men and took a moment to survey the scene in front of him. They had completed their project of building the Rhino Ferries, the flat-bottomed pontoon barges to be used in the upcoming invasion. Many bobbed and swayed in the water in front of him.

The Rhino Ferries, powered by two 143-horse power Chrysler outboard marine motors, measured one hundred seventy-five feet long and could hold forty vehicles and up to six hundred tons, their strength equal to a civilian highway bridge. During the invasion, soldiers, trucks and tanks would be able to unload from the ships onto the ferries and cram into every available inch for the trip to the landing beaches.

One of the Seabees' mottos, "Can Do!" was perfect for my father, who was tall and strong and enjoyed getting things done.

His Scandinavian heritage and his childhood growing up on a farm had taught him the meaning and value of hard work. He enjoyed being an engineer, using his mind to design and create real and practical things in the world, bridges, roads, water systems and in this case, ferries.

His light blue eyes reflected his kind nature. At twenty-nine, he was considered "old" to the young sailors of eighteen, but they looked up to him and valued his engineering knowledge. He and his crew had been working long hours for months to prepare for the invasion.

Everyone was anxious now to get going; the waiting had put the men on edge and decreased morale. Evenings they gathered in the neighborhood pub to drink warm beer, even learning some of the local songs. Dad whistled one of the tunes as he walked back to the barracks, "I've got sixpence, jolly, jolly sixpence, I've got sixpence, to last me all my life…"

He was proud of the work he and his men had done to build the ferries. Eisenhower had just given the word for the invasion. They were ready.

June 6th, 1944

The stormy weather made the trip across the English Channel cold, wet and rough. But this was it. My father and his men felt the excitement and importance of being a part of the Allied invasion of France. No one slept that night as the boats crossed the choppy channel; they drank strong, hot coffee to stay awake. Dad and his crews had been assigned to land at Omaha Beach; the other Americans would land on Utah Beach, further west.

The bad weather created more problems than just rough seas. The early morning air strikes missed their targets above Omaha Beach, due to thick storm clouds. But no one knew that until it was too late.

Just before dawn, when the first landing craft arrived on Omaha and soldiers spilled out, the Germans opened fire. The strong seas sank twenty-seven out of the twenty-nine tanks that were supposed to help; the soldiers who were not dead or wounded had no cover from the German fire on the flat beach.

The second wave of reinforcements encountered the same withering gunfire. In addition, the high waves and strong currents took the landing craft off course; soldiers were not able to land at their assigned sectors, creating even more chaos.

After hours of this disastrous scenario, a Naval destroyer pulled in close and blasted the cliffs, blowing up some of the German bunkers. In addition, by late morning, a few brave soldiers scaled the hill to take out the Germans behind the guns. By nightfall, after a day of brutal fighting, the beach was relatively secured.

The next morning, when my father and his men made the trip to the shore, rows of bodies lay on the beach, waiting to be identified as the tide rushed in and sea gulls swarmed, screamed and dove.

There were no words for that horrific scene. Dad, an officer, felt like an older brother to the young sailors of eighteen who were under his command. Some of them were vomiting, others crying as he struggled to keep his own composure. "War was hell," the saying went, and this scene was about as close to hell as he could imagine.

He thanked God and fate that he and his men had not been assigned to land the previous day and said a prayer for those young men lying there who had lost their lives and their futures the day before.

He had worked with his men for months in England and knew that if they could focus on the projects ahead, it could take their mind off this nightmarish scene. Their Rhino Ferries, called by some a "secret weapon," had been a huge success in getting troops and heavy equipment from ship to shore on D-Day at a speed both unprecedented and unanticipated by the Germans.

One of the Seabees' mottos was, *"Construimus, batuimus,"* "We build, we fight" and their mascot, a feisty-looking bee, carried a drill in one hand and a gun in the other. The Seabees had their work cut out for them again. They had to transform the beach and the cliffs beyond into a major staging area for the next crucial phase of the war. Three million troops would land there in the coming months. The success of the war depended on it.

There were the roads to carve out from the beach up to the campsite on the hill and beyond, the camp and the airstrip to build. The soldiers needed hot showers, the cooks needed mess tents to prepare meals and the doctors needed the infirmary set up and supplied.

In addition, there was the continuous job of unloading the huge supply ships daily, crammed with the material of war—the gasoline, tanks, Jeeps, guns, ammunition and medical supplies, not to mention the thousands of tons of food needed to feed the men.

German planes strafed the beach, snipers' shots rang out and there was the constant danger of stepping onto one of the thousands of land mines hidden everywhere in the rough, grassy earth or on the beach. Dad carried a standard military issue 38-caliber pistol on his belt. He had earned a medal for sharpshooting, but his job was to build first, then to fight.

He and his men had a job to do and they would do it, "on the double."

2

Seven-year-old Gilbert Des Clos sat in the tall grass on the cliff above Omaha Beach and shivered in the sea air. The sun rose over the trees as he hugged his bony knees tight to his chest and pulled his worn, wool sweater around him.

Ever since the arrival of les Américains weeks before, his world had changed. Overnight, a military camp had materialized on the empty field just below his home in Normandy. For Gilbert, an orphan, it was a boy's dream. His caretaker, Madame Bisson, had to drag him in at night.

Now he watched, wide-eyed, as Jeeps roared up the road and men in white caps scurried about, emptying trucks loaded with guns, ammunition, food, and giant duffel bags. He yawned as the smell of bacon, eggs, coffee, and toast wafted up from a massive tent. As he tilted his small head back, breathing in the aromas, his stomach growled.

My father held a clipboard and checked off the morning's accomplishments. The infirmary tent was complete; now the medics and doctors had a decent place to treat soldiers. The showers worked and the hot water had raised morale.

He and his men had been busy since dawn; it was now noon. He dismissed them, then took a moment and touched the breast pocket that held the photo of my mother and their two young sons. It had been so long since he'd seen them and he hadn't received a letter in weeks.

When he turned to go, he spied something moving in the tall grass on the hill. He tensed and his hand moved instinctively to the gun on his belt. But he paused, knowing they had secured this area, and peered into the grass. He thought he saw a head. Was that a child?

He lifted his hand in a wave. A small hand waved back. It *was* a child. Dad paused, then beckoned. There was a moment of hesitation, and then a boy, barely taller than the grass, made his way down. Dad knelt to look into the child's thin face.

The little guy looked about five years old; his worn, brown sweater had holes and barely covered his bony torso. His legs stuck out like sticks from his baggy, tan shorts. Dad wondered where he had come from and thought he looked like he could use a good meal. At least they had plenty of food—in fact, they threw out a lot each day, and he was determined to do something about that when his turn came to oversee the mess tent.

The boy's clear blue eyes twinkled as he smiled, then looked down. Dad searched his brain for the French that he'd been reviewing. He'd thrown his high-school French book into his wooden sea locker when he found out he was going overseas and had studied it on the ship and some evenings since the landings, when he wasn't too tired.

Dad knelt down and tried out some of his words with Gilbert.

"*Comment vous appelez-vous?*" No, he corrected himself—this was a child and you used the familiar form of "*tu.*" "*Comment t'appelle-tu?*" he asked. What is your name?

"*Gilbert,*" pronounced "Jeelbeert," came the soft answer, barely audible.

"*Moi, je m'appelle Donald, Donald Johnson.*"

Gilbert smiled as Dad shook his hand.

"*As-tu faim?*" Are you hungry?

The smell of roast beef, carrots and potatoes, apple pie and coffee drifted out of the mess tent and mixed with the fresh sea air. Other officers rushed past into the tent and Dad felt his own hunger pangs. He'd eaten breakfast at 0600. Church bells in the nearby village rang out the noon hour.

"*Veux-tu déjeuner avec moi?*" Do you want to have lunch with me? Dad asked Gilbert.

Gilbert nodded his head, so Dad took his small hand and led him into the officers' mess tent. Once inside, he picked the boy up and jiggled him a little, like he always did with his sons at home. Gilbert giggled and hung on, then his eyes became wide as he took in all the food spread out in front of them. Dad took a tray and filled a plate for himself and one for Gilbert.

During lunch, Gilbert kept his head down, eating his food with relish, but from time to time, peeked up and smiled. It looked to Dad as though the child hadn't eaten that well in years, if ever.

Dad talked to the other officers, discussing the plans for the afternoon: who would oversee the unloading of the ships, which group was going to continue on the project of camp construction and distribution of the newly arrived sea bags and mail for the enlisted men.

But he kept looking over at Gilbert, who sat close by. As he watched the boy eat, he patted him on the head and smiled at him. "*Très bien,*" he told him. Very good. Gilbert smiled back.

When it was time to get back to work, Dad led Gilbert outside, knelt down again and tried to remember what else he could say in French. He managed to say that he had to work, but invited Gilbert to return that evening at dinnertime, 1800 hours, six o'clock.

Dad got into his Jeep to head down to the beach and paused to look back. Gilbert stood in the same spot, watching. A soldier walked by and saluted Dad. Gilbert raised his hand in a salute, giggled and then ran up the path and out of sight.

My father sighed. The little guy was so cute and he had gobbled up his lunch. Then the work of the afternoon ahead pulled him back and he sped off to oversee the unloading of the ships that had pulled in with the high tide.

With a difference of over forty feet between the low and high tides, they brought the huge ships in at high water. Then at low water, with the ships high and dry, they could open up the front end and unload directly onto the beach. Each day, the Seabees landed hundreds of thousands of tons of war material.

They had to stay alert, though. The tide rushed back in at a speed "faster than a galloping horse" and once it reached the ship, they couldn't move fast enough to close the ship's hull back up and to get everything to high ground. They had lost tanks, Jeeps and supplies under the water a few weeks before when Dad left someone else in charge and he wanted to make sure that it didn't happen again.

At 1800 hours, Dad walked toward the officers' mess tent. He'd showered, the warmth of the water relaxing his tired muscles, and had changed into a clean uniform.

Gilbert stood where they'd said goodbye earlier. The same old sweater and shorts, the same shy smile. Dad took his hand, then hoisted him up and headed into dinner.

The menu was fried chicken, mashed potatoes, corn, biscuits with butter and chocolate cake. Gilbert didn't eat as much as he had at lunch; it was clear that he wasn't used to so much food. But he sat close to Dad and smiled his shy smile, taking big breaths between bites, as if willing himself to eat as much as he could.

After dinner, Dad knelt close to Gilbert. "*Bonsoir,*" he said. "*A demain.*" Goodnight. Until tomorrow.

He watched the boy scamper up the path and out of sight.

As the days and weeks of the summer of 1944 passed, Gilbert blossomed, his skinny body filled out and his cheeks became plump and rosy with the summer sun. The comfort of the hot meals in the officers' mess tent, seated next to Dad, assuaged his physical hunger, but the time and attention Dad gave him strengthened him in other ways. He lost some of his shyness. He smiled, laughed out loud sometimes and giggled often, especially when Dad carried him around on his shoulders.

Gilbert soon began riding along in the Jeep down to the beach, when Dad supervised the unloading of ships. When my father oversaw construction projects in the camp, Gilbert tagged along. If Dad left camp with his crew to rebuild a road or a blown-out bridge, the boy waited at the gate for his return.

My father's French improved, and Gilbert learned to say "hello," "goodbye," "thank you," "Jeep," "ship," and "ice cream." He could also say, "Lieutenant Donald Johnson."

The other officers and soldiers enjoyed including Gilbert in the life of the camp. In fact, the boy seemed to help ease their homesickness. But Gilbert's favorite was Dad. Dad began to piece together that Gilbert lived nearby in a house with another child, Georgette, and her grandmother, Madame Bisson. He was an orphan, with no parents and no family.

Dad had known that war would be brutal and it had been. He'd lived nightmares that would haunt him for the rest of his life. But in the midst of all that horror, there had been this gift, this little boy, who had become a part of his daily life. He found himself wondering about Gilbert's future. He began to wish he could somehow take him home to America.

Late one September afternoon, Dad drove his Jeep into the nearby city of Caen where he had heard there were some governmental offices. Winding through the bombed out streets filled with rubble, he found the tiny office. With a French dictionary in hand and some sentences he had written out the night before, like French homework, he asked the man behind the desk if he could apply to adopt a French orphan and bring him back to America.

Even with his limited French, he understood the response. *"Non, ce n'est pas possible."*

He'd argued, trying to understand the more extended explanation, but just couldn't follow what the official was saying.

Defeated, he steered the Jeep back to the camp, his shoulders slumped from the disappointment. He'd grown to love Gilbert and knew that the boy had grown to love him. He had hoped Gilbert could just be added in to his family.

My mother hadn't been thrilled, writing that Dad should come home and get to know the two sons he already had. But he pleaded with her in his letters and over the months, she gave in, since he felt that strongly.

It all had seemed possible. Now he had just been told that it wouldn't be. But surely, there must be a way.

Dad knew that when his orders changed, saying goodbye to Gilbert would be painful. He was determined that the time he had left in France be as rich as possible with the boy.

On the long evenings, some of the officers organized football or softball games. Dad had played some softball in college and was a good, strong hitter. Gilbert sat on the sidelines and watched, clapping and smiling when Dad hit the ball with a thwack and ran around the bases.

One night, Dad decided Gilbert should have a chance to play. He led him to home plate, stood behind him and together they held the bat. When the ball hit the bat, Dad swooped Gilbert up and they raced around the bases. All the men played in slow motion, making sure that the pair made it into home plate. Gilbert beamed with excitement when everyone cheered at their success.

In early October, as the days began to shorten and the wind off the sea became cold, Dad and his crew drove to Bayeux to repair a bridge. In the quaint village, many of the shops remained intact. Among them, Dad saw what looked like a children's shop, *Le Petit Bateau*, the Little Boat.

Once the work of the morning flowed smoothly, he put a junior officer in charge and walked over to the shop. The bell on the door tinkled a cheery greeting as he opened it and went in. The lights had not yet been restored to the building and it was dark inside, except for the dim light of a gas lamp. But the elderly woman in the back smiled and came forward with a cheery "*Bonjour.*" He smiled back and tried to explain what he was looking for.

"*Pour un garçon.*" For a boy. He held up his hand for Gilbert's height and gestured to establish the boy's slight frame. Dad pointed to his own shirt, pants, and to a sweater he saw nearby. The woman bustled about, opening drawers and ruffling through shelves, then walked over to the dusty window to show him some tan shorts, a light blue shirt and a dark blue sweater.

"*Très bien,*" Dad exclaimed and pointed to a package of clean white underwear.

"*Et les souliers?*" And shoes?

When Dad nodded, she asked, "*Quelle taille?*" What size?

Dad paused, then estimated Gilbert's shoe size with his hands. The woman searched through the shoeboxes that were lined up along a sidewall, mumbling to herself in French, then brought out a pair of brown leather shoes that looked to be just about right. And a pair of brown socks to match.

"*Et un chapeau?*" she asked.

"*Mais oui!*" Dad replied.

She produced a wool beret, dark blue to match the sweater. At the last instant, he grabbed a small stuffed bear that was propped up on a display.

As Dad got the Francs out of his wallet and paid for the clothes, the proprietress wrapped them up in brown paper and tied the parcel with string. He whistled as he left the shop, calling out "*Merci, au revoir,*" to the owner. She returned the greeting and waved.

Back at the camp, Gilbert waited, smiling and waving when Dad pulled in. As soon as Dad was free, he grabbed Gilbert and swung him up onto his shoulders. He told the boy that he had a big surprise for him, but first there was something they had to do. Dad walked over to the showers tent and explained to Gilbert that he wanted him to take a shower.

"*Non!*" Gilbert exclaimed in horror and fear, trying to run away. He had never been inside the shower tent or taken a shower and howled like a frightened, trapped animal.

Dad knelt down, took Gilbert's shoulders and looked into the boy's eyes.

"*Gilbert, Gilbert, calme-toi.*"

Dad explained that after the shower, Gilbert would get his big surprise, in the brown packet, tied up with the string. Gilbert sniffed and hiccupped, his small mouth puckered into a pout, but he let Dad take off his worn clothes and coax him to step under the warm water. Dad motioned for him to use the soap, to wash his face, and behind his ears, then his hair, then wrapped him up in a towel to dry.

When Dad opened the brown parcel and showed the clean little boy the new clothes, Gilbert gaped.

"*Pour toi,*" Dad said.

Gilbert stared, his mouth open, then began to shiver, still staring, unmoving.

"*Allez.*" Let's go. Dad helped Gilbert to put on the clean, new underwear, then the shorts, the shirt and the sweater, the socks and shoes. He'd done well with the sizes. He toweled the boy's hair, popped on the chapeau and handed him the bear. When Gilbert saw his reflection in the one long mirror in the shower tent, he danced and smiled, turning round and round, laughing at the little boy in the mirror. Dad bundled up the old clothes in the brown paper.

While Dad showered and changed into a clean uniform, Gilbert kept wiping off the steam so he could stare in the mirror, making faces and turning to see himself from all sides. At dinner, he smiled his shy smile, hiding a little behind Dad, when other officers admired his new clothes.

Later, Dad held Gilbert's hand as he walked him up the path to Madame Bisson's house and handed her the package of the old clothes. She gasped and frowned when she saw Gilbert in his new finery. Gilbert waved from the door and said goodnight.

The next day, however, when Gilbert came down the hill to meet Dad, he was wearing the old worn sweater and tan shorts and looked like he was about to cry. Dad stared at the boy in disbelief.

He handed his clipboard to the next in charge and told him he'd be right back, then took Gilbert's hand and marched back up the hill and rapped on the door. Madame Bisson opened it and scowled. Dad motioned to Gilbert, put his hands on his hips, and narrowed his eyes. Gilbert hid behind Dad.

"*Et où sont les nouveaux vêtements?*" he demanded. And where are the new clothes?

She shrugged, then disappeared into the dark house. When she reappeared, she had the clothes wrapped up in the brown paper again, tied tight with the string.

"*Maintenant, je vous attends.*" Now, I am going to wait, Dad barked, crossing his arms across his chest and tapping his foot. She reached for Gilbert and yanked him into the house. A few moments later, Gilbert reappeared, white-faced but wearing the new clothes and holding tight to the bear.

"*Merci,*" Dad said through clenched teeth and held the boy's hand as they went back down the path to the camp. From that day on, Gilbert appeared each morning wearing his new clothes, with the bear tucked into his pocket or inside his blue sweater.

In late October, the air turned crisp as the days shortened and bright red apples fell off the trees all over Normandy. Cows grazed on the dying grass and farmers gathered what they could from their trampled fields. The area felt again like the peaceful farming region it had been before the invasion. Paris had been liberated August 25th and all the fighting had moved east, pushing the Germans back toward Germany.

Dad had hoped to get a chance to visit the "City of Light" before he left France, but the rebuilding work that the Seabees performed was so needed that he never managed to get the leave to go.

His orders had changed and his battalion was leaving, to head back across the English Channel and then to make the long sea voyage home to America. He hid that fact from Gilbert, trying to put off the painful news as long as possible.

But the day of departure, when Gilbert saw Dad's empty tent and wooden sea locker by the door, he burst into tears.

"*Non,*" he screamed. "*Non!*"

Dad knelt down and pulled the boy close. Gilbert buried his head in Dad's thick, wool Navy coat, sobbing. Sailors bustled by, heavy sea bags hoisted onto their shoulders, laughing and excited to be going home. A pair of sailors pulled up in a

Jeep and hoisted Dad's locker up.

This was how it had all started, he thought, as he held Gilbert on the dry grass outside his tent. He'd knelt down and met this little guy just four months before. Now Gilbert was a part of his life. As he patted the boy and tried to soothe him, he felt his own tears in the crisp October wind.

"*Sois fort,*" Dad said in a husky voice. Be strong. "*Tu dois être fort maintenant.*" You have to be strong now.

As men hurried by, heading for the ship and home, Dad held Gilbert for as long as he could before the final moment of goodbye.

Part II

1953

3

My father is dreaming. He's thrashing and mumbling and waving his arms. I'm four and am standing by his bed, waiting. It is fall, 1953 and he's been home from the Korean War for a few months. Because it is a Sunday morning, I know he'll read me my special book. I don't know what he is dreaming about, but I sense that he is far away. I touch his shoulder.

"Daddy, will you read me my story?"

I clutch my favorite picture book, *The Golden Egg*, about the duck that hatches out of an egg with a rabbit standing by. I can't read yet, but I've looked at the book so many times that the binding is starting to come apart and the shiny clear paper on the front is peeling off.

Behind me, my parents' two imposing mahogany chests of drawers stand against the sidewall. A large statue of St. Joseph reigns on Dad's dresser, the Virgin Mary on Mom's. On Dad's, there are also a set of keys, coins in a small leather purse and one of my finger paintings from kindergarten—red and blue swirls with a purple heart in the center, my small fingers evident in the movement of the paint.

I love that painting. That was the moment when I discovered that red and blue combined to make purple. I gave it to my daddy and was proud that he had it on his dresser.

He's sleeping in an undershirt and jockey shorts, his usual sleeping attire. I'd seen it sometimes at night, when he got me up to go to the bathroom, patted my back when I was throwing up or comforted me through a nightmare. In summer, when the one-hundred-degree heat made it hard to sleep, he often stood by my bed, raising and lowering the sheet, creating a cool breeze, till I fell back asleep.

"Daddy, will you read me my story?" I touched him again.

He opened his eyes and looked at me, but his glassy eyes looked right through me. He was somewhere else. I waited. We'd done this before. I knew he'd come back to me. He sat up on one arm and shook his head, blinked his eyes, looked around the room and then at me. Then he smiled at me and I could see in his eyes that he was back.

"Of course. Of course I'll read you your story."

He patted the space next to him, stretched, then threw the pillow back so that he could lean on it against the green plastered wall and I could snuggle against his broad chest.

"Sit right here and we'll read your story."

I hopped up, holding my book tight against the front of my faded cotton pajamas with the blue flowers on them. In some vague and undistinguished way, I sensed that I was a link back into this life, a child he loved, from wherever he'd been in his dreams. I didn't know that in the world of his dreams, another child he loved called out to him, reaching out his arms.

I didn't know yet about Gilbert.

I snuggled close, listened and giggled as he acted out the antics of the duck hatching out of the egg, in his deep voice.

Then he carried me into the yellow kitchen, jiggling up and down as we walked till I giggled, and set me down at my place at the table for a bowl of Wheaties or Ruskettes. Gradually, everyone wandered in for breakfast before we left for Mass.

In my small world, the yellow kitchen, like the rest of our

house, seemed huge. Years later, when I went back to visit, I saw that it wasn't that large. When we first moved in, the walls and cabinets got painted a shiny, cheery yellow.

New linoleum, beige with brown flecks, covered the old pine floors. The hope was that the linoleum pattern might hide the dirt that four children, playing outside all the time tracked in, even with the best of intentions.

We moved to the big and rather spooky old house when my dad was overseas in the Korean War. So crowding into the kitchen together probably made us feel safe, without him with us. Then, throughout my childhood, the kitchen and the yellow Formica table remained the hub of the household and of our lives.

My parents met by chance in 1940, when my father, who was working at his first engineering job in Helena, Montana, happened to go to a dance after a basketball game on a frigid February night. My mother, on a trip from Australia and visiting Helena, also attended that dance.

There must have been a great physical attraction between them to blind them to their differences. It wasn't just their nationalities that set them apart.

My father, born in 1914, the middle of five sons, grew up on a farm in South Dakota and put himself through the South Dakota School of Mines by working nights in a printing shop. His whole life he'd worked hard, going to bed early and getting up early. His mother, a loving, gentle and kind farm wife, cooked, canned, and raised a big vegetable garden and chickens.

My mother was born Daisy Catherine Bonnye Finch in 1915 in Sydney, Australia. A year-and-a-half later her father deserted the family, just before her mother gave birth to a second daughter. My mother grew up being told that her father was dead. Her mother's father, a successful businessman in Melbourne, took care of them. Mom was sent off to a Catholic boarding school at age eight, so spent most of her childhood with nuns. There are photos of her making her debut at eighteen in a long white gown.

When she, her mother and sister made the six-week voyage to America in 1939, they traveled on a luxury liner. She smoked, drank and liked to stay out late partying. When she met my father, she had never made a bed or cooked a meal.

In spite of these differences, or perhaps ignorant of them, after a whirlwind courtship of less than three months my parents were married at the Catholic Church in Missoula. They are a handsome couple in their wedding photo from that day, innocent of the challenges that lay ahead of them.

But they had problems from the start. My mother had no real experience with men, growing up without a father and being taught by nuns. My father had no sisters, there were no women in his engineering classes and he couldn't have married a woman more unlike his own mother if he had tried.

My brothers, Kenton and Clark, were born in quick succession, then World War II came along. With Dad's training and being overseas, first in Europe and then in the Pacific, the war separated my parents for over two years. After the war, my sister Sharon and I joined the family, part of the post-war baby boom.

At that point, my mother had four children, ages seven, five, two and a newborn. I don't have any memories of being held or cuddled by my mother. In the one photo I have of Mom holding me when I was a baby, she is holding me up and away from her, not cuddling me close.

There was the washing and ironing, the cooking and cleaning and the shopping. To my dad, all that work would have seemed normal, after what his mother had done on the farm.

So if my mother complained, he may not have listened with a sympathetic ear.

The tension between my parents was the air that I breathed for as far back as I can remember. My mother was angry with my father and she was angry with me for being close to him. And it got worse over the years.

Once I was old enough to toddle around, I joined the pack of older siblings, especially Sharon, who was just twenty-two months older than I was. So for a lot of years I was buffered from my mother by being the youngest member of the boisterous brood and by having my sister and father there.

But at the same time, when my dad was away at work or gone, when I was alone with my siblings and mother, many times I felt left out. My mother and my brothers were close, having spent time as a family unit when Dad was gone in the war.

My mother favored my sister and there was a subtle inner circle of my brothers and sister that I was not let into by Mom. Nothing was said overtly, but I couldn't gain access there and it frightened me.

Life felt like a precarious experience. Except when Dad was around. I knew I was safe then. But that just seemed to infuriate Mom more. I was caught up in an invisible web and I couldn't find my way out.

Dad loved to tell the story of how as a toddler, I sat on the front porch of our house and waited for him to walk up the hill from work. Still in diapers, I wore a cotton dress and sturdy leather shoes.

When I spotted him, I jumped up and toddled off down the front path, past the brown weeds, which should have been a lawn, and turned right onto the main sidewalk. As I headed down the hill, my chubby legs picked up speed, going faster and faster. He swooped me up into his arms just seconds before I could have toppled over onto the hard cement. When he told me the story, he swooped me up again, just like he did then and I'd squeal.

Being the youngest meant I was always the shortest, slowest, least coordinated of the bunch, clamoring to keep up. But when my dad hoisted me up in his strong arms, then I was at his eye level, all 6'2" of his tall frame, meaning I was not only way higher than my siblings, I was higher than most of the other adults in the room, even my mother.

Dad moved through space with power and speed—later on we'd run to try to keep up. So when he carried me, I could move along at his pace—now that was an advantage. I remember how it felt to be held in his arms, close to him like that. Even if he was busy with others, talking, he let you know that you were welcome there.

He told me that one time when he was leaving on an airplane, the roar of the propellers frightened me and I clung to him shivering. But when I realized he was getting on the plane, I said, "I'll go with you Daddy."

Just after my third birthday, December 1951, Dad's Seabees unit was called up to go overseas in the Korean War. There's a photo taken on the day he left, in front of our house. He's wearing his dress Khaki uniform and Sharon and I are hanging onto either side of him. I was not smiling. I knew he was going away and what would I do without him?

Then he got into the back seat of a car and the door closed with a thwack. I'd never seen my daddy in the back seat of a car, with someone else driving. He looked out the window and waved as he pulled away. I watched the car disappear down the street until it was gone.

I turned into my sister Sharon and cried, the cotton of her school uniform scratching my face. She didn't move away from me, but just let me cry. After a moment, she took my hand to walk away, but I kept staring down the street. Maybe if I stood there long enough, he would come back?

My father was gone a year and a half. While he was away overseas, we moved into a large, old house outside town on Chestnut Drive, on three weed-filled acres interspersed with orange, grapefruit, tangerine, lemon and plum trees and sur-rounded by avocado groves.

The house had been an old people's home, run by a nurse; the shabby and dingy rooms had numbers over the doors. Somehow the numbers came down and the smell of fresh paint replaced the smell of sick, old people. Sharon and I explored all the nooks and crannies, a little spooked out at how large it was after the tiny bungalow we'd always known as home.

The size of the new place made it fun for hide-and-go-seek, with so many rooms to explore. One day, as Sharon and I played, I snuck into my parents' closet to hide. I hid in the farthest corner on Dad's side, tucked in back behind his blue plaid flannel bathrobe that hung down to the floor.

As I waited in the dark, close space, I could hear Sharon counting from one to a hundred. Then her "ready or not, here I come," and the sound of her footsteps on the wood floors as she ran around searching for me.

I waited, scrunched into Dad's robe, breathing in his smells and that of his shaving lotion, Aqua Velva. At first, that felt comforting, the familiar scent of him, there in the closet, from his robe. But then, the next moment, I felt a stab of pain. *Oh no, my daddy is gone. Where is my daddy?*

I pushed aside the clothes, gasping for air and burst out of the closet just as Sharon rounded the corner, her face full of expectation and fun. I threw myself down and curled up into a ball, wailing, "Where is my daddy?" Sharon knelt down next to me, a bit stunned.

"What happened?" she asked.

I sat up and pointed at the closet, a horrified look on my face. "D-D-Daddy's robe, it smells like Daddy," I said, wiping my tears and hiccupping.

"Oh," she said, looking solemn as I flopped down on the floor again, whimpering. She sat close to me and I could see her orange checked shorts out of the corner of my eye and could feel the skin on her bare leg next to my face. It was too hot to go outside in the hundred-degree heat that day and we'd been trying to break up the boredom with this game. She patted my head.

"Yeah, I miss him too. But don't let Mommy hear you. Shh, shhh. She'll be mad, remember?"

I remembered the hard slaps I had received for crying that I missed my daddy. I breathed hard and traced the lines of the hardwood floor with my finger. It was September 1952 and my father had been gone for almost a year. I wanted to scream and cry but that would only get me into more trouble. Sharon sat with me till I calmed down.

Dad came back from Japan and Korea the following July 1953. My first memory of him being home was at the Yellow Formica table where he was handing out the gifts he'd brought back for us.

He was *home*. I'd thought maybe that I had imagined his loving presence, warm hugs and deep laugh. But there he was again, calling me Diane Mary, holding me tight and smelling like Dad. I wanted to hang onto him, but knew I'd be in trouble with my mother for that, so sat in my chair and trembled with excitement. I couldn't eat, so pushed my food around on my plate. Luckily, that night, no one noticed.

Sharon got a wind up doll with a pretty pink dress and also a kitten that batted at a just-out-of-reach butterfly, suspended on a wire. I got a wind up, brown, furry monkey that clapped cymbals. There were Japanese comic books, fascinating in their foreignness, and my brothers got shiny bright jackets. We learned to count to ten in Japanese:

Ichi, Nee, San, Shi, Go, Roku, Shichi, Hachi, Kuu, Juu.

Dad said we learned in five minutes what it took him months to learn. Dad also brought a set of Noritaki china back with him, which became our "good" china that we used for holidays. Mom never liked that china. She didn't come right out and say it, but from her forced smile or pursed lips when she looked at it or talked about it, you could tell. I thought it was very pretty—white with little pink and purple flowers all over it. But she liked English bone china and it was clear that this china, from Japan, was not as good.

I learned to live with the unspoken contrasts all around me. My mother's anger, my father's love, the tension between my parents. I found solace in my sister Sharon's soothing presence and the freedom and fun of playing outside with her, running through the orange groves fragrant with spring blossoms.

On a hot summer day, we'd grab one of the sweet oranges that hung low on the branches, suck the warm juice out of it, then rinse off our sticky hands and faces at a nearby faucet.

We didn't have many toys, but instead busied ourselves outside making little villages in the dirt under the mulberry tree, where it was shady and cool. We spent hours building houses made of twigs and bark, carving roads in the dirt and digging swimming pools, complete with a stick diving board. I watched fascinated as the ground absorbed the water from my pool and would keep refilling the tiny dirt hole with a cup, from the faucet.

My small world opened up wide when I went off to kindergarten, at age four. There, I was not the youngest child trying to keep up with three older siblings and the world was just my size. Each morning, between nine and noon, I could feel how I was a separate, independent person, a tiny space ship of thoughts and feelings and so much joy.

We played in the little house with the miniature stove, pots and pans, and the table and chairs for a certain time in the morning. Then followed another delight—music time or playground time or milk and graham crackers.

They read us stories, like my daddy did, and I felt my brain swell with the words and images. And then finger painting on giant easels, the wet, sticky feel of the paint on my fingers. That clean white paper was all mine, to fill up with color, swirls of red, then blue and then, oh wonder of wonders, the two colors overlapping into a burst of purple.

There was so much to learn and to do in the world. The teachers helped and encouraged us and seemed to want us to enjoy ourselves. I wasn't bothering them by my presence.

4

Mom and Dad had agreed on at least one thing, to raise us in the country. So Dad drove forty-five minutes each way down a two-lane road to the Department of the Navy in San Diego where he worked as a civil engineer. For many years he made the commute on an old Indian motorcycle he bought cheap and restored, taking her apart and putting her back together till she shone and purred.

He was so proud of that motorcycle and called her his "ancient Indian." Even before I could read the big round clock on the wall in the kitchen, I could tell the time each evening by the roar of Dad's motorcycle coming up the driveway.

That was a signal that it was five forty-five, time for Sharon and me to stop playing paper dolls or dress up or to come in from outside and set the table for dinner, with the yellow plastic Melmac dishes and the stainless steel silverware, a white paper napkin folded under each fork.

At six o'clock sharp, our family of six crowded around the yellow Formica table. Dad and Mom sat on each end, my sister across from me at Dad's end, our older brothers next to us, at Mom's end. We recited the Catholic grace together, "Bless us our Lord, for these thy gifts, which we are about to receive, from thy bounty, through Christ our Lord, Amen."

Next to Dad, at his end on the back inside wall, he'd built a narrow, wooden shelf for the toaster. He kept it going all during dinner, passing around whole-wheat toast slathered with margarine to try to fill up the four growing children gathered around the table.

The menu rarely changed——meat and potatoes, cooked frozen vegetables, salad with avocado and the toast. Our glasses of whole milk came from Hollandia Dairy, our local dairy just across town. The milkman left the wire rack of frosty bottles on our back porch three mornings a week. When you popped the cardboard top off the milk bottle, thick cream gleamed on the top. For dessert, there might be canned peaches or fruit cocktail in heavy syrup and sometimes cookies.

But to get dessert, I had to clean my plate. And I hated those frozen vegetables, especially the lima beans. The yellow vinyl and chrome chairs that matched the table had food scrunched into the places where the chrome met the vinyl. Some of that food was my vegetables from previous dinners.

Dad's childhood on the farm during the Great Depression taught him the value of food. He loved to see us eat. At the dinner table, he told the same corny jokes and stories over and over. After dinner, he fogged up his glasses by blowing steam from his coffee cup, then looked around and asked, "Where'd everybody go?" I laughed so hard I got the hiccups.

On the nights that we ate chicken, he liked to tell the story of how, when he was a boy, his mother Signe, would pronounce, "Donald, go get me a chicken." This chicken would pay the violin teacher, Miss Larson, for four weeks of Dad's lessons.

Dad had created a little trap with a bent wire, so he could nab a chicken at the neck, lead it off to the side and chop off its head. He didn't like that part, but raising animals for food was a part of farm life. He then walked the mile to the violin teacher's house, with the freshly plucked chicken wrapped in thick, brown paper tucked under one arm and his violin case under the other.

Dad loved his violin lessons, but he had to practice out behind the barn when his father, Bernard, was busy in the fields. Bernard, a powerful man of strong Danish stock, stood 6'4" and thought that violin playing was for sissies.

So Signe, who loved music, poetry and books, paid for the lessons with her one source of cash, her chickens. She also sold and bartered her eggs for fabric to make quilts and for store-bought soap that smelled like lavender.

In my mind's eye, I could see my dad, moving the bow across the strings and listening for the notes to sound right as he sent them up to the sky behind the barn. Perhaps his mother heard him as she shelled peas on the porch or busied herself at the stove, cooking large meals for five sons and a husband, all hungry from farm chores. Maybe she smiled at Dad later, letting him know that she had heard his music.

Dad's voice always softened when he talked about his mother and said her name. Signe had only completed the third grade; she was needed on the farm to help with the younger children and the chores. But she could figure out Dad's complicated high-school algebra and math problems when she helped him with his homework.

I could feel my grandmother's strength in Dad's stories, especially in how she went against my grandfather to give Dad those music lessons. Dad even played the violin for me once, the song "Little Red Wing" and I could see from the way that he swayed with the music that the violin still meant something to him.

But then my mom made a snide comment and I watched as he put the violin back into its case, closed it with a snap and put it on the top shelf of the closet. I never saw him take it down again.

Dad talked about how he and his brothers walked to Pioneer School, a rustic one-room schoolhouse where students sat at wooden desks with inkwells in the right-hand corners, used an outhouse for a toilet and carried in wood to stoke the woodstove. Winters in South Dakota get down to thirty degrees below zero. On those days, his mother would hitch up the wagon and drive them to school.

Many times, as Dad overheard the lessons of the classes several years ahead, he'd blurt out the answers, then receive a frown from the teacher. He never learned cursive writing, except to sign his name, but developed a style of fine, neat printing.

Back at the yellow Formica table, Dad used to say, "If you can't eat, you're sick." That was usually true in our house, when the only time you didn't show up at the table to eat was when you were lying sick in bed.

Some nights, during dinner, he talked about his time in France during World War II. "Eat your vegetables. The people in France didn't have enough to eat during the war." He liked to tell the story about how it upset him that they used to throw out left over food at the Navy camp. He knew that people were hungry nearby—the farmer's fields had all been trampled in the fighting and during a war, there were shortages of everything.

"So when it was my turn to be in charge of the mess tent, I loaded up a Jeep with pans of steaming hot meat, vegetables, bread, butter, pies—whatever I could find. Then I drove down the narrow lane from the camp and stopped at a farmhouse, knocked on the door, gave them a pan and said, *"Pour vous."*

His eyes lit up at this point, remembering what happened next. "Oh, the French people cried, smiled and shook my hand, speaking so fast that I couldn't keep up with their French. But I understood their gratitude."

He'd stop for a moment, take a sip of his coffee, savoring those memories.

"Each night, I went to a different farmhouse and was greeted with such warmth and surprise. I looked forward to that time at the end of the day. It felt like being Santa Claus." That made me giggle.

"But then, when I no longer had that duty, the next person in charge just started throwing out the food again. I tried to explain what I had done, how easy it was and what a difference it made. But they just looked at me like I was nuts."

He shook his head at that memory. From all the times I listened to that story, I could see it all in my head, Dad in the Jeep with the pans of food, the farmhouses down a narrow lane and the French people, waving their arms in excitement.

A story that always made me laugh was when Dad described how his high-school French teacher had never learned French, so would study to stay a chapter ahead of her students. She'd also never *heard* French and taught them with a midwestern accent, so *sucre*, sugar, came out sounding like *soocray*.

"So on a day when I was taking a break from unloading the ships, drinking a cup of coffee and eating a roll, and a Frenchman walked by and nodded, I'd smile and want to try out my French. I'd hold up my sugar packet and say, "*soocray, n'est-ce pas?*"

Dad always paused there, and I'd hold my breath, knowing what was coming next.

"The poor Frenchman would look puzzled, then peer at the sugar packet and realize that I was trying to say *sucre*. "*Ah oui*," the man would nod and exclaim—"*oui, sucre!*" Dad would then say it like it should have sounded, kind of like *sooke*.

"Then I'd point to a pad of butter and say, "*la booray, n'est-ce pas?*" The Frenchman would frown, then brighten up and beam, "*oui, le buerre*," which sounded like *le burr*, and we'd laugh, a moment of understanding between us." I could tell that Dad's French improved greatly from these encounters.

Dad also liked to tell fables, like "Chicken Little," how the mother hen planted and grew the wheat to make the bread, did all the work, with no one helping. Then, when it was time to eat the bread, everyone wanted to share it. I liked those stories too. All Dad's stories lived together in the soft spaces of my imagination, his life on the farm, France, French people and "Chicken Little."

I first heard the story of Gilbert at the yellow Formica table. Dad always said the boy's name with a soft G sound, the way the French said it, *Jeelbear*. Not Gilbert, with a hard G.

He talked about how Gilbert had looked hungry, so he had invited him to eat with him at the officers' mess tent. On rare nights, he talked about how he tried to adopt Gilbert and bring him home to America. But he didn't elaborate on that.

"Clean your plate now, eat your vegetables. You know, Gilbert Des Clos didn't have enough to eat during the war. He would have been happy to eat those lima beans."

I stared at the pale green lima beans, cold now because I had pushed them around my plate for so long, hoping to create some kind of magical vortex that they would disappear into. *Poof.* But they didn't disappear. They stared back at me like big, pale green eyes, and my dad would not give up.

"Hold your nose, close your eyes, chew and drink some milk real fast," Sharon suggested. She was keeping me company while the lima beans and I waited each other out. I'd already squished two into the space between the yellow vinyl chair seat and the silver chrome chair back rails. But there were five more left. Dad was firm.

"They're good for you," he said. So I took a breath and ate them up fast, nose held, eyes closed and milk swallowed.

"Good job. You may be excused." Dad smiled. I gagged. Sharon giggled. But it was done.

Who was this Gilbert Des Clos, the French orphan boy who would have gladly eaten those lima beans? I knew he was different. First of all, he was *French* and that meant that he spoke those soft musical sounds that were not English. He was also different because he wasn't there with us, but was part of the stories that my father told about his time in France, way back before I was even born. So was Gilbert really real?

But my father always told the truth, so it must have been true that Gilbert had almost become my brother. But where would we have put him at our very crowded kitchen table? I already had two elder brothers and wasn't so sure I wanted another one. We had two boys and two girls, even numbers. Gilbert would have tilted that over to three and two.

And the idea of another big boy around seemed like too much. They liked to burp loud, tease my sister and me and wrestle and punch each other. No, not another brother. I don't think my mother wanted another child either. She already seemed like she had too many. And she never said anything about Gilbert when Dad talked about him. Her silence seemed to say that she hadn't been that excited about it.

"What happened to Gilbert?" I'd asked. Dad didn't know and the look in his eyes changed when I asked him that, so I learned not to ask again. But still I wondered. Gilbert didn't have a Daddy like I did. And he had almost had my daddy. That must have been really hard for that little boy so far away.

I didn't know that it was also hard for my dad, right there at the table with me, telling me to eat my lima beans.

5

Mom had shortened her name to Bonnye Finch John-son, started a consignment shop called "Bonnye's Outgrown Shop" and was gone on Saturdays. My brothers already had jobs working in people's orchards, so Saturdays, Daddy was in charge of Sharon and me. We probably had mismatched tops, bottoms and socks, our hair may not have been combed, but oh did we have fun.

Dad always had a long list of things to fix in our 1917 vintage house—and there was plenty to do—old rusty pipes that squirted water and scary looking frayed wires that crisscrossed in the attic. Growing up on a farm, he learned to tinker and knew how to fix anything—cars, houses, plumbing and wiring. I thought all men could fix things.

As Dad worked, Sharon and I stayed close by. If he needed a part for one of his repairs, we all headed off to a junkyard, where he searched around in rusty bins. Sharon and I explored through aisles of bathtubs with orange stains around the drains and giant claw feet, and old toilets and sinks on their sides, clustered together like little families.

Since our mother took the car to work, we rode behind Daddy on his Indian motorcycle for these errands. Sharon hung onto Daddy's back, and I hung onto hers, leaning into the curves to the roar of the engine, hair blowing wildly. The blue sky moved past through the trees like a kaleidoscope, if I turned my head up to look. It was good to feel my daddy, sister and me all linked together as we whizzed down Tenth Avenue, turned right onto Juniper Street and then left at the hanging traffic light at Grand Avenue.

Back home, at lunchtime, Dad had a limited cooking repertoire, so lunch was always fried spam sandwiches. Our job was to toast the bread and slather it thick with margarine, while he fried up the spam, which sizzled and popped, splattering grease all over the top of the electric range. Then he slid a thick slab of spam onto the bread.

"Spam sandwich, comin' up, hot and juicy and made to order," he exclaimed as he cooked. Then we sat together at the yellow Formica table, eating our sandwiches, the grease dripping down our hands and agreeing about how yummy they were.

It was on one of those Saturdays that we spied the small carnival.

"Can we stop, Daddy? Oh look, there's a roller coaster," Sharon said.

I wasn't sure what a roller coaster was but I saw some small cars, kind of like a train. I liked toy trains.

"Okay, sure we can stop, for a treat," he said. He pulled the Indian motorcycle over and parked.

In the seat next to Sharon on the little train, I saw the hill up ahead. *Uh oh.* The man took our tickets.

Daddy stood by the fence, smiling and waving as the train started to move. We edged up the hill, click, click, click, click, then were at the top of the hill and I could see ahead. *Oh no, what was this?* We headed down.

Sharon squealed with delight, but I shuddered and

shrieked, hiding my head on her shoulder. As we raced past Daddy, a blur against the sky and trees, I screamed "Daddy get me offff!" And then he was gone.

Click, click, click, click. I looked back, my face white with fear and my voice high-pitched, "Daddy, get me off!" We headed down the hill again and around back towards the man with the big metal crank that turned the ride on and off, and Daddy.

As we sped by him again, I saw Daddy talking to the man, in a loud voice and waving his arms. I heard "right now" as the train car rushed past again, then the loud screech of brakes and we were stopping, just short of the hill. By this time I was huddled into Sharon's side. Then Daddy was standing there, holding out his arms.

"It's all right. I've got you."

He lifted me up and out and to the other side of the fence. The man turned the big crank and the train started again. I stood next to Daddy and hid my head into his pants leg and plugged my ears against the sound.

Sharon whizzed by, a blur of excited screams and smiles. Daddy patted my head, then knelt down and put his arms around me. I shuddered with relief that I was safe from that monster climbing up and barreling back down the hill.

First grade, at St. Mary's School, we sat two to a wooden desk, with a hole on the right hand corner where an inkbottle used to go and the initials of many former students carved into the tops. Learning to read was a joy. The squiggly lines on the page became letters and the letters became words that I could read.

"See Jane run.

Run Jane run.

See Spot go. Go Spot go."

I took home my reader and read to my dad and he was so proud. And then later, I could read fairy tales for hours and hours, transported to other lands with handsome princes and beautiful princesses, castles, dragons and so much magic. And happily ever after. That was a new concept for me, that people were happy and then stayed that way "ever after."

Except for with Sharon and with my Daddy, there was not a lot of happy in my house, and with my parents, there was no "happily ever after."

As much as I liked school, learning numbers, letters and learning to read, I felt frustrated. When were they going to get to the *real* questions and the really important answers?

Such as, 'why aren't my parents happy? Why does my mother hit me and always seem so angry? Why does my daddy look sad and sigh? How does a person get happy and stay happy? Why do people kill each other in wars? Why is Father Mitchell fat if there really are starving children in China? He could send them some of his food.'

But no one asked those questions or even hinted at the answers. Each year I returned to school excited. Maybe *this* year they were going to answer those questions and the many others I'd been thinking about? But each year I watched my hopes being dashed again.

In my first memory of a standardized intelligence test, we had to match up the pictures that went together. There was one in particular that I remember. The choices were paper, scissors, a tree and another item. I drew a line with my pencil from the paper to the tree, since paper came from trees. When the nun went over the answers with us, the *correct* answer to that question was to match the paper with the scissors.

"But wait. My answer is also a good answer," I raised my hand to say.

"No, that is not the *correct* answer. The correct answer is *scissors*," she repeated, scowling and turning her back on me so that the long veil she wore on her head made a swishing sound, letting me know that there would be no more discussion on the subject.

At that moment, I saw that there was more than one way to see things and that even if she scowled at me, I *liked* my answer and my way of thinking.

In the third grade, my father drew a large multiplication table on cardboard for me, so I could see it all written down, and see how the numbers were all spatially related to each other.

When I walked to school and carried the chart under my arm, it went all the way down to my hand. At mass before school, I had to rest it between the kneeler and the back of the pew in front of me.

I loved that chart. I saw math in it, the concepts, the numbers and their relationships. I saw my father's love too, how we sat together at the yellow Formica table as he drew it out for me, the numbers clear and straight.

Then the wonder of how I learned it by heart because I could see it all in my head. 7x9=63, 8x8=64. The nines were hard, the tens and elevens easy and then it was done and I knew it. I was the best in my class at multiplication.

That was before I learned that girls weren't supposed to be good in math or science. Just boys.

When I brought home my report card from St. Mary's School, I stood by Dad's desk, as he read each line out loud, his voice full of admiration.

"Reading A, Mathematics A, Religion B-." (I asked too many questions there about God and the saints and why and how do we know for sure…)

"Social Studies A, Penmanship, B."

"Gets along well with others, E, citizenship S." (I day-dreamed sometimes.)

I'd shiver and glow, feeling so seen, loved and appreciated.

"I'm very proud of you, Diane Mary," he'd say, his blue eyes twinkling as he smiled at me. "Keep up the good work." Then he'd sign the card with a flourish, *D.K. Johnson.*

6

There's a wire recording from when I was about four and I'm singing, "Sing a Song of Sixpence a Pocket Full of Rye." As I sing the words "parlor" and "clothes," I have an Australian accent. Mom must have taught me the song and I mimicked her accent.

By the time I went to school, I knew my mother was different. For one thing, she sounded different. Her voice had a clipped and commanding sound so unlike other children's mothers. "Oh no dear"—pronounced "deaahhh," she'd say.

She drank tea and coffee out of fine English bone china teacups that had to be washed and dried very carefully, chain-smoked and had a sophistication that seemed mysterious and foreign.

I knew that she came from somewhere else, "down under," so far away that it took people weeks and weeks to arrive by ship. I looked on the globe in our living room and it was so far away, it almost wasn't on the globe at all.

In moments of exasperation, which were many with four wild American children, she'd exclaim, "You don't speak English, you speak *American*!"

She said zed instead of Z, naught instead of zero and when I came home from St. Mary's School in the third grade and told her about the American Revolution, the Boston Tea Party and the brave American patriots, she became agitated and incensed.

"Oh no, you have it all wrong! They were the ungrateful colonists!" she sputtered.

I knew then, at age eight, that history was made up according to what side you were on and that in her childhood, her country was *not* on the American side.

She wore high heels and wool skirts and sweaters when other mothers wore pedal pushers and sneakers. She was tall, strong, opinionated and loud and loved to wear big hats. Many times I was embarrassed by how different she was, wishing she would just blend in with the other mothers, who made cookies and smiled sweetly. My mother didn't blend and rarely baked cookies or smiled sweetly.

When we watched Queen Elizabeth's coronation on a tiny black-and-white television in 1953, she cried when they played "God Save the Queen." I saw something then—that she had a past that I wasn't a part of, from a place that I didn't know. Seeing her cry also made an impression on me. Her softness and vulnerability in those moments cut through her usual cold and aloof exterior.

In our small kitchen, the ironing board stood right next to the table and a lot of the time Mom was ironing when we were doing our homework. That's when I realized she said zed for z and naught for zero, or heard about the ungrateful colonists.

That's also when I heard the stories of her childhood in Australia. Tales of how Mom helped the maids and butlers polish the silver for fun. Or how Mom went on a cruise to Fiji, at age twelve, by herself, on a school break. She even showed us the silver eggcup that was a souvenir from that trip.

These stories landed with about as much reality as the fairy

tales I loved in my thick and heavy *Grimm's Fairy Tales* book—
"Hansel and Gretel" and "The Twelve Dancing Princesses." My
mother at boarding school, helping maids and butlers or alone
on a cruise fit in there just fine.

Whenever a blue airmail letter arrived from Australia, we
knew to leave her alone. She sat at the table, cigarette burning
in an ashtray, head down over the letter, silent as she pored
through its contents. She finished and started again, sometimes
reading it three or four times, wiping away tears or staring off
into space. Her utter concentration was stunning, her silence
intimidating. Unless someone was bleeding or had started a
fire, we left her alone.

There was a world within those fragile blue pages with
squiggly lines on them, a world none of us were a part of. It
was a place she was connected to that we weren't, a way that
she was separate, not our mother. I was both fascinated with
and afraid of that world.

She was hard enough to reach and understand as it was. At
those moments, I lost her completely. A few times, the heavy
black telephone in the hall jangled and a crackly voice, with an
even stronger accent than my mother's asked for her.

We knew that those phone calls from across the planet
meant that someone had died or there was some bad news
that couldn't wait the several weeks it took for a letter to arrive.
Something had happened in Australia, the place so far away, to
someone we didn't know.

Birthdays, we received a blue airmail letter of our own or a
brown packet tied with string containing a delicate hankie or a
pair of socks. We had to sit down at the yellow Formica table
and compose a thank you note to Nana Finch, a grandmother
we'd never met and thank her for the hankie or socks.

I didn't use hankies and the socks were usually too small;
our large American feet rarely fit into them. Clearly Nana Finch

had a vision of us as dainty and polite Australian-speaking children, who raised their pinkies while drinking tea from china cups. But that didn't match the reality of the loud, boisterous brood of four American children that we were.

One day, while drying the dishes, when I was about seven, I broke one of Mom's English bone china cups. She screamed at me, her face red with fury, her lips pursed to keep her cigarette dangling from the corner of her mouth, the smoke twirling up around her head.

"How could you be so *stupid?*" she fumed.

I knelt down to pick up the broken pieces of the cup from the floor, trying not to cut myself and noticing how they clicked and clattered against each other in my shaking hand. As she raged and yelled, I made a vow to myself: When I grow up, I will never do what she is doing. I will never make things more important than people.

Things break and go into the trash. But when people break, they carry their broken pieces around, looking for ways to put them back together again.

My mother was like a simmering pot, ready to boil over at any moment. She was stewing in her own pain, but I didn't know that then. When she screamed and pointed down at me, her whole body quivering with rage, "You should be ashamed of yourself," I believed her.

A lot of days, I didn't know what I had done. We were in the kitchen, where it seems we nearly always were. She was at the sink or the ever-present ironing board or at the stove, a cigarette burning between her lips. When she started to yell and stomped over to the broom closet in the corner, I knew what was coming.

She grabbed the yardstick or the belt that hung on a nail and headed for me. When I was little, I didn't move, just felt the stick or the belt on my back, arms, legs and rear. Later, I tried to run, but when she caught me, she hit that much harder.

I learned to take myself away, to go inside behind my eyes, to not be there with her distorted red face, the pain on my body, and the sound of her cutting, angry words. Mothers were supposed to be nice to you.

And why was she only mean to me, not to my sister and brothers? There must be something wrong with me. It must be my fault. But then, why was my dad nice to me? He didn't treat me like something was wrong with me.

I learned to read her energy, to know if I was safe or not. Sometimes she felt neutral. I liked neutral. One time, I remember scurrying across the kitchen and she grabbed me and put a bobby pin in my hair to keep it from falling into my eyes.

She'd been cleaning out a drawer full of S&H green stamps, rubber bands from the *Daily Times Advocate* newspaper, pencils, paper clips and bobby pins. The ever-present cigarette and the smoke curling above her head looked the same, but she felt safe that day.

I loved that moment of being seen by her and touched, even if it was just with a bobby pin. She might have even smiled at me. There were some good moments with her, too. Moments that made the painful ones worse, because I felt close to her, just for a while.

When I was about eight, I remember going to a special church service alone with her. It was evening, some kind of a holy day. Candlelight reflected off the brick walls of the crowded church and the air was thick with smoke and the sweet smell of incense as the priest droned on in Latin.

We stood to sing a song. This was special because we didn't usually sing in Mass. I knew how to read by then, so Mom pointed out the words for me. The refrain was "Everlasting is thy reign."

I stood close to Mom. She had come home from work, so had on high heels and a skirt, more dressed up than the people around us. When she sang, I could hear her accent, "Ever-laaahsting is thy reign."

That moment, I felt her difference. But I also felt, *this is my mother, with her high heels, her accent, her otherness.* I might have moved a few inches closer to her, into her side and under her arm that held the hymnal. She might have let me.

Just for the moment. Just for that one moment.

At night, after putting on my cotton JC Penney pajamas and brushing my teeth, I climbed into my single bed, pulling the pink, cotton quilt from my grandma Signe up around my neck. I'd only met that grandma once, but felt her caring through all those hand-stitched threads in my quilt and where she'd signed her name in dark pink thread, *Signe Johnson, 1954.*

Sharon's bed was a few feet away from mine, but my bed was against the outside wall. I scrunched up against the cold plaster, trying to hide under the windowsill. That way, when the boogieman looked in, he wouldn't see me. He would see Sharon and that worried me, but I didn't know what to do about that. I'd already checked under the bed to make sure there were no monsters hiding there. It was all clear, for now.

One night, I lay awake, tense and restless; Sharon was already asleep. I chewed on my fingernails until they hurt. That was going to get me into more trouble with my mother, but I couldn't seem to stop. I hugged my teddy bear tight and squeezed my eyes shut, hoping that would bring sleep.

When I woke up later, the house was quiet, which made the scratching on the window just above me that much louder. I could hear Sharon's quiet breathing in the next bed, then the scratching. I shivered. Should I look? What was doing that scratching? When I sat up to look, I saw a monkey at the window, looking right in at me and screamed out, in terror.

"Daddy, Daddy, there's a monkey at the window!"

I yelled as loud as I could, then covered my head with my quilt, so the monkey couldn't see me. I heard Daddy's footsteps coming down the hall, then the squeak of my bed springs and felt the sag of my mattress when he sat down on the edge of the bed. I heard his soothing, calm voice through the covers.

"Shhh, shhh, what's the matter Diane Mary?"

"There's a monkey at the window, scratching the glass," I whimpered. "I saw it, looking at me."

"Come on out now and let's look," he said.

I peeked out from under the quilt. He smiled at me and pointed to the window.

"No monkey, see? Just tree branches and leaves scratching the glass. Go back to sleep now. No reason to be scared."

He patted my back and sat with me as if he had all the time in the world. He acted like it didn't matter that I'd awakened him in the middle of the night for an imaginary monkey at the window. I went back to sleep feeling safe, at least for that moment.

During the day, I loved to run and play, skip and whoop, thrilled to feel my heart beating fast and my muscles getting stronger as I grew, able to keep up better with my sister and brothers.

"Don't get overexcited," my mother said often, in a sharp tone, frowning with a deep furrow between her brows. I didn't know how to say, I'm *not* overexcited; this is my natural state, and besides, excited is good.

One day, coming home from playing hard with a friend, I stuck my sweaty head out the back, side window of the pink 1950 Studebaker. The cool breeze on my damp forehead and scalp sent a thrill through my body.

I also loved to breathe in the fresh air and not my mother's cigarette smoke, which filled up the car. Then the sharp reprimand and my head yanked hard back into the car, with a slap on the arm.

"You're going to catch pneumonia doing that. Close that window now," my mother snapped, from the front seat. I cranked the window back up and watched as my body heat steamed it up in seconds.

Who cares, I thought, as I drew faces on the steamy glass. And what is p'monia anyway? I just want to feel that fresh air.

I had been sick for a week, allowed to sleep in my parents' bed. The doctor came to visit, with his stethoscope and black bag, shook his head and talked in a low tone to my parents. Sharon peeked around the corner. I was not getting better. I was just so hot.

I woke up in a hospital bed, alone. A doctor and two nurses hovered around me. They were forcing a tube up my nose and the pain cut like a knife. I rose up out of my delirium, pushed them away and yanked it out, stunning everyone, mostly me. Until that moment, at age eight, I had never had any power over what adults did to me.

The doctor looked shocked, but I was determined to not let them hurt me like that. I lay back again, exhausted. The three of them whispered at the end of my bed. A young nurse in a starched white cap came around to the side. She had kind blue eyes and blond hair tucked under her cap and she took a moment to look right at me, smile and pat my hand.

She explained that they wanted to get a culture from my stomach so that they could give me a vaccine to help me to get better. She asked me to swallow a tube, while drinking some cold juice.

"It might feel a little funny but it won't hurt," she said.

I nodded yes. She came back with the juice and helped me

to sit up and drink it while I swallowed the tube. It was just like she said—it felt a little funny, but it didn't hurt. She smiled at me again and patted me on the head.

"Good girl," she said and I knew she meant it. I went back to sleep.

My father had been sitting by my bed every night after work. I saw him for brief moments when I woke up but was always too tired to talk to him. One night, his voice pierced through my stupor and I heard him pleading with the doctor and nurses.

"You've got to do something. You can't just let her lie there."

"There is one new drug, but it is experimental," the doctor said.

"Use it. Do it now," he thundered.

I knew he was there, trying to pull me back from where I was floating away to. A little later, they helped me to sit up to swallow a pill, then I fell back into the bed.

"It could take some time for it to take effect," the doctor said.

I could just make out my dad in the chair next to the bed as I drifted off again. The voices and my dad seemed so far away, but I could feel him there with me.

When I woke up again, I was hovering above the bed. I could see the hospital room, the single metal bed, the wood floors, and the table with the glass of orange juice with the red plastic bendy straw. My father sat in the metal chair and his head dropped forward every few seconds, then jerked back up, then down again. It was the middle of the night and he was dozing.

I saw my small, unmoving body, showing barely a bulge in the bed. But wait. I was up above that bed, looking down. And I felt like I was drifting away, being pulled by an invisible tide.

It felt all dreamy, cocoon-like and warm, but different from the feverish heat in my body. Soft, blurry even. I saw a glow behind me and then I looked back at my daddy. He was there, along with the lump in the bed and that glow beyond the hospital wall. I was floating right through the wall, so easy, toward that golden glow.

But wait. Stop. Hold on just a minute. I was *leaving* through that wall. I couldn't leave through a wall. Something was really wrong here.

I looked back at my daddy, nodding forward again and thought of sitting in his lap, looking at a book, or having a piggy-back ride when I could hear the change jingle in his pants pocket.

But this floating. Did this mean that I was dying? I had heard about dying, where people go away and don't come back. A little girl in my class drowned in a boating accident; she was there on Friday and didn't come back on Monday. She never came back. Maybe this is where they went, toward that yellow glow on the other side of the wall, where I was going.

I felt so free. It would be so easy. But what about my daddy? He would be so sad. He would never forget that I had died. I looked back at him again in the metal chair.

And wait. I'm only eight years old. I don't want to die. I haven't even lived. I want to become a teenager and wear those big poofy dresses that teenage girls get to wear to dances with boys. I want to become a grown up and go out into the world and drive my own car and do what I want.

I don't want to die.

I opened my eyes and blinked at the bright sun shining through the window of my hospital room. I wiggled in the narrow iron bed and felt the starched white sheet against my thin bare legs. The nice young nurse was looking down at me, smiling and her eyes were very bright blue and filled up with water.

"There you are now. There you are. Welcome back."

Her voice sounded husky and she brushed my cheek with her soft hand. My throat felt so dry that the insides of my mouth stuck together and I couldn't talk.

"Here, I brought you some nice cold orange juice. It will make you feel better and help you to get strong again."

She held it out for me and helped me to sit up. I drank a few sips, swallowing carefully as the dryness eased. I could hear my mother's voice out in the hall and the click of her high heels on the polished wood floor. Her Australian accent made her words sound clipped and sharp, irritated. But the familiarity of it felt comforting.

My mother is here. I am here. I laid my head back down on the pillow feeling very tired and closed my eyes. I'd had the strangest dream. Daddy was in it and a golden light. I'd been floating away, through that wall over there.

But now I was back. It felt like I'd been gone a long time. The nice nurse said that I'd had pneumonia and had been in the hospital for more than a week. When I heard the word "p'monia," my stomach clenched tight. I would be in trouble with my mother. It would be my fault for sticking my head out of the window.

For the p'monia.

7

My mother sold her outgrown shop and began working at a travel agency, which allowed her to earn a free ticket to Australia. In the summer of 1957, she was returning to her country for the first time since 1939 and bringing back her mother, Nana Daisy, to stay with us. Our grandmother would also stay with our aunt, my mother's sister, who had also married an American and lived nearby in San Diego.

Dad took that chance to pack up all four kids to travel across the country to his family reunion over the 4th of July in South Dakota. He'd only gone back a few times since he left in the late 1930's and we kids had never been.

We had a Lincoln Capri, a long, sleek white car that Dad had bought used. Whenever we needed a "new" car, he disappeared for the day, returning with a different car at day's end, one he could pay cash for with the trade-in. Mom was never pleased with his purchase. She wanted a new car.

The day he came home with the Lincoln Capri, I went out to look and passed Mom on her way back to the house, scowling and taking fierce puffs on her cigarette. I missed what had she said to Dad, but could see the effect of her words.

He stood by the car with his head down, staring at the ground. I climbed into the back seat and jumped up and down while Sharon slid in on the other side.

"Oh Dad, nice soft seats. And electric windows—can I try?" He turned the engine on and Sharon and I each made our windows go up and down, amazed at the "whir" sound that meant that the window was moving without someone cranking it hard.

"We'll have a lot more room in this car, for all six of us. We won't be so crammed," I added.

Dad smiled at our excitement. When it was time to make the trip to South Dakota, he took out the back seat, laid our old, mismatched and scratched suitcases down, then put a worn, pinstriped mattress on top, covered with a faded sheet. Sharon and I were to have the back seat, with Dad and the boys up front.

My two brothers were fifteen and thirteen and excited about being able to drive some on the long stretches across the country, away from towns—and cops. Sharon and I settled in with three comic books and some pillows on the mattress.

Dad figured out our route so that we stopped and camped in National Parks, like Yosemite, Bryce Canyon, and Yellowstone. In the trunk, a green, tattered, canvas army tent, five army-issue down sleeping bags and five air mattresses got stashed.

When we stopped for the night, ropes, stakes, poles and canvas turned into a tent, then Dad and my brothers raced each other to blow up the air mattresses. At dark, we all crawled in and squished together.

I discovered the wonder of Yosemite, my first time ever seeing a rushing river, huge granite cliffs, and pine trees reaching high into the sky. We swam in the icy cold river, shivering next to the campfire after to get warm, but excited and happy. Each day we arrived at a new place to explore, even if it was only for one night.

Dad handled meals by streamlining the process. Dinner was Dinty Moore Beef Stew heated in the can over the open fire, served in tin cups. Breakfast, those same tin cups appeared, with canned milk diluted with water, poured over Wheaties. Sharon and I complained loudly, especially when the menu didn't change from day to day. But we were so hungry we had to eat it. That was all there was.

Lunch consisted of sandwiches made along the side of the road, peanut butter and jelly, or sometimes a package of lunchmeat gobbled up in one sitting. We didn't have a cooler. Food preparation was not Dad's strong suit.

The sun burned through the back windows of the Lincoln Capri, and the hours dragged by. Sharon and I got bored back there rolling around on the old mattress. We passed some time singing along to the radio, loud. Elvis Presley, singing "Jailhouse Rock," "That'll be the Day," by Buddy Holly and the Crickets, "Bye Bye Love," or "Wake Up Little Suzie," crooned by the Everly Brothers.

But my small world expanded day by day in the National Parks, with the scent of pine trees, fresh mountain air, and the sound of a river rushing by. Even the stinky geysers at Yellowstone where I clung onto Dad, afraid I'd fall into those bubbling pools, were interesting and exciting. Dad had never seen the National Parks either, so he relished the experiences too.

Once, he stopped at a dam, being the civil engineer, and we all trooped out to see. I didn't like dams, I decided, though I didn't say anything. I'd just seen my first wild rivers and the idea of damming one up and stopping that bubbly, free flow seemed wrong.

On the last day we drove and drove, pulling into my grandparents' farm late at night. Over the next week, we met aunts, uncles, cousins, and even my ninety-year-old great-grandfather. The sixteen cousins ranged in age from babies to teens with Sharon and me in the middle at ten and eight. The adults sat around visiting, and we kids raced past, playing tag or hide-and-go-seek. We all lined up for the group photos, the shortest in front.

I loved the organized chaos of it and so many people who felt like my dad, warm and openhearted. It felt special to see where he had grown up, to sleep in the room he slept in as a child and to be with his mother and father, on the farm. I'd met them once or twice, but only at our home, where there was an unspoken tension and strain with my mother.

Here, people laughed and told stories and they loved my dad. At home, Dad went by Don or D.K., but his family called him Donald. Dad and his brothers lined up with their arms around each other for special photos of the "boys." Dad's youngest brother Lester had died in a plane crash five years earlier. There were choked voices, even some tears, at all being together again, without him.

Sometimes, as I'd race through, one of them would grab me and exclaim, "Oh Donald, she's just like you." Those words felt good in my ears and in my heart.

My grandma Signe stood 5'1" tall, tiny next to grandpa Bernard who was even taller than my dad. Grandma wore a flowered cotton housedress, a white apron, and sturdy black shoes, with her gray hair tied up in a bun. I was already almost as tall as she was.

I crept downstairs into her cellar one day and when my eyes became accustomed to the dark, saw shelves and shelves lined with quart and half-gallon mason jars filled with fruits and vegetables. There were loaves of fresh-baked breads and pies lined up like a bakery. She must have worked for months to get ready for this reunion.

Grandma Signe didn't say much to me, but the look in her

eyes was soft and gentle. She loved to grow flowers, in addition to tending her huge vegetable garden, her chickens and her cats.

On that trip, with Dad and his family and with Mom gone, life felt different—peaceful and safer. When we visited my ninety-year old great-grandfather, his gruffness made me so nervous that the top of my one-piece sun suit accidently fell into the toilet as I was using the bathroom. When I came out to tell Dad, he didn't yell at me or spank me. He just took off his shirt and gave it to me to put on, not at all upset that he was left just wearing his undershirt.

"We'll hang it on the line back at the farm. Don't worry," he said, patting me on the head and holding me close as he said goodbye to his grandfather. Sharon and I giggled at how Dad's shirt hung down and became a dress for me.

After our visit to the farm, we faced the long ride home, the boredom in the car and more camping. My brothers drove and Sharon and I read comics as America passed by the windows of the Lincoln Capri. But I'd learned that I had a whole family of warm and loving people, just like my dad, who thought I was special. I'd felt the warmth of my grandmother's love. I tucked it all away inside of my heart.

My mother returned from Australia with her mother, Nana Daisy Finch, a short, stout, gray-haired woman who smelled like baby powder, wore a corset and spoke with such a strong Australian accent that we barely understood her. Her presence added to the already busy and chaotic household.

Her cooking skills consisted of knowing how to boil an egg, make a cup of tea and a piece of toast. Because of a slight stroke, she walked with a cane, so couldn't help with cleaning and I'm not sure she knew how to clean. She was not at all like the strong grandmother I had just met in South Dakota.

Our mom had been working on and off since we started

school, so Sharon and I learned to come home from school and start dinner, following Mom's hand written instructions. "Brown meat on both sides in bacon grease. Turn down to simmer. After one hour, add peeled potatoes and carrots and some beef broth. Continue to simmer." Nana Daisy didn't help with that either.

Mom took the car to work, so Dad still rode his motorcycle to his job in San Diego each day. I remember one night going out to meet him in a drizzle. I heard the roar, meaning he was coming up the driveway and watched, as the single headlight got closer in the dark, wet night. The rain streamed off his bright yellow rain suit as he pulled in and parked.

But when he got off and turned towards me, the way that he stood and the look in his eyes seemed peaceful and invigorated. He must have loved those forty-five minutes each way, alone with his thoughts, the wind roaring past, the sun coming up in the morning or the hills becoming shadows as the sky turned dark in the evening. It was his time away from the chaos of four boisterous children, one angry wife and now her mother.

Dad still told his stories at dinner, about France, the war and Gilbert, and I felt comforted by the familiarity of it all, even though so many other things were changing around me.

My parents argued a lot about money, so we knew that money was tight, though no one ever told us that outright. Dad did say, "Money doesn't grow on trees" more than once.

Dad's prize possessions were his Argus C3 camera, his movie camera and the wire recorder, which lay hidden in the solid wood cabinet, also containing the radio and record player. The Argus camera required getting a reading with a hand-held exposure meter, like "f-16 at a 60th of a second," all the things that cameras do automatically now.

Then he had to stop and set the camera to take a picture. At night, he had to replace each flash bulb after it popped, one at a time. There was no such thing as a spontaneous photo.

At family gatherings, Dad commanded us to "line up and walk towards the movie camera," which we did. Then he hopped in, giving the camera to someone else, walked towards it and waved in a kind of salute. We have a lot of home movies of his relatives from the Midwest, standing by the orange trees, smiling and looking amazed at the dangling orange fruit. Sharon and I wondered what the big deal was. Didn't everyone have orange trees?

At special school events and recitals, Dad marched right up front, juggling the movie camera and the Argus like a journalist. He wanted to get those photos of his children and he did—he didn't care what other people thought of him. *That's my dad*, I'd think when I'd spot him up in front, flashing away with his camera. I might have acted embarrassed, but inside I was proud of him.

On Christmas and birthdays, we gathered around the wire recorder and Dad "interviewed" us. We found ourselves with a microphone stuck in our face, trying to think of something to say. But it was a special treat to later listen to those crackly recordings of our voices describing things that were already in the past. It gave me, at a very young age, a sense of time passing by.

Dad sent the rolls of photos and movies away to be developed and when they came back after a week or two, we had a "movie night." He set up the white screen at the end of the living room, and got the heavy movie projector and the slide projector each set up on a chair. While he was busy dropping the slides into the canister, we made rabbits against the light on the screen or any other shapes we could think of.

It was fun to sit there in the dark together, watching pictures of something that had happened weeks and even months before and that we had already forgotten about, pictures and movies of us smiling and acting like a happy family. For those brief moments in the dark, I could even pretend that we were.

Part III

1961

8

Sharon and her best friend Holly huddled close together on Sharon's bed discussing their first day of high school, fall 1961. I was still in the eighth grade, eager to hear about their new world.

They talked about all their classes—biology, chemistry, and for Holly, French I. Sharon had to take Latin. My mother insisted that it was the "mother of all languages" and that we all had to take two years. Mass was also still said in Latin. Sharon read from her Latin I book. I was unmoved.

Then Holly began reading from her French I book, words and phrases like *chambre meublée*—furnished room. She tilted her head and made her lips into a kissing shape, "*Oui, oui, chambre meublée.*" She and Sharon giggled; I was transfixed.

It sounded exciting, hypnotic and worldly to be able to make those French sounds. Holly said, "*Je t'aime.*" I love you. I sighed. How romantic. I kept listening, my attention riveted on the sounds and on my own sense of excitement.

I'd heard French words before, when Dad talked about his time in France during the war, but Dad's French sounded Midwestern, American, boring. This French sounded luscious, sensual, inviting.

That day, that moment, those sounds, may not be something that Sharon nor Holly would even remember. But as I sat there, on the soft chenille bedspread in the bedroom of my childhood, something inside of me woke up and paid attention.

I could learn those sounds and words and be a part of that place in the French I textbook, with the side walk cafés where starving artist types sipped strong coffee out of tiny cups. I didn't know what starving artists were and I had never tasted coffee, but I sensed that if I went to this place, where they said *chambre meublée* like that, I could be happy.

I could also be far away from the small town where I'd lived my whole life, far away from my mother's coldness and anger. I could even visit some of the places Dad had been during the war. If I learned French, I could disappear into this country with the Eiffel Tower and castles. It seemed like a fairy tale and a fairy tale sounded good right then.

The next year, my freshman year at high school, I suffered through the dreaded Latin I class—*amo, amas, amat, amamus, amatis, amant*, the conjugation of the verb 'love' in Latin. I was unmoved. The teacher, Mrs. Vogel, had taught both my brothers and Sharon and looked like she was old enough to remember the days when they still *spoke* Latin. I had the class right after lunch and struggled to stay awake.

I longed to study French. My best friend Susan had started German and I so envied her learning a *real* language. I had never forgotten my excitement that day on the bedspread when Holly had read out the French words. I wanted those sounds. So I begged, pleaded and cajoled my mother into letting me out of Latin after only one year.

"I could take French," I argued, a language that people still spoke. Didn't that make more sense? My mother actually listened to me and I prevailed. I could start French my sophomore year. Goodbye to Latin forever! I couldn't wait.

The next year, Sharon and I began French I together; I was a sophomore, she was a junior. It was a first for us to share a class, and we sat next to each other, and chatted before class. But once the bell rang, I was riveted on the French. That first year, our egotistical teacher enjoyed hearing himself speak French in a pompous voice, but gave an easy A or B if you were a girl and smiled at him. I did that, but also earned my A+.

My junior year, my second year of French, Sharon and I moved into Mr. Maiwald's class. He was a short German man with a pointed head and one eye that didn't move. He also had the reputation of being the hardest teacher in the school, and flunked students regularly. Next to my dad, he was the smartest person I'd ever met.

Mr. Maiwald made it very clear on the first day that he would give hard tests, be a tough grader, but that we would learn French. I was thrilled. I became obsessed. I made flash cards by writing French vocabulary words onto "3x5" index cards and carried them with me wherever I went. I studied them on the half-hour bus ride to and from school.

I put them on the ironing board so I could learn new words when I ironed my starched white gym shirt and dark blue gym shorts each week or the blouses with the big ruffles down the front. I stayed up late studying and figuring out all the tiny nuances of how the verb endings had to agree when you conjugated them, all of the different tenses, all the accents and irregular verbs. I knew he was going to ask those things on the exams. But it wasn't that. I had to learn it all for myself.

French and my dream of going to France became the center of my own private universe. In it, I was safe from my real life as a teenager, from problems with my mother, from boyfriend woes, from worrying if I was fat. When I said those sounds in my head to an imaginary French person, *"Bonjour, je m'appelle*

Diane," Hello, my name is Diane, I felt free and alive.

I scored 100% on all the tests. It became a sort of silent battle between us, this short, stocky German man with one funny eye and this tall, shy, high school coed. He wanted to see if he could make me stumble. He never did.

Excelling in his class felt exhilarating. Each word I learned, each rule I mastered, and each accent aigu or accent grave I correctly placed on a French word became a small victory. It took me another step closer to my dream of flying across the Atlantic Ocean to France, sitting at one of those sidewalk cafés and moving my lips like a kiss to speak French.

My senior year, in French III, I worked harder than ever. Mr. Maiwald spoke only French in class, so I was good at understanding but still shy about speaking it.

The big house felt empty with my sister away at college and my brothers grown up and gone. By this time, my mother barely talked to my father. She had moved into my brothers' empty bedroom at the other end of the house.

Still, the three of us still sat down to dinner most nights at the yellow Formica table, eating food that I prepared when I got home from school. One night stands out in my memory. Dad asked Mom about her day.

"Fine," she answered, not looking up.

He turned to me and repeated the question.

"Fine," I answered.

In the silence, our knives and forks scraped against the yellow Melmac dishes. Then I heard my father sigh and I glanced up at his face. His normally sparkly blue eyes looked dull and his shoulders slumped. I noticed his plastic pocket liner in his shirt with his pen and slide rule sticking out; he had just come home from work.

He looked lonely and sad. Why was I treating my father

like this? I felt ashamed that I was hurting him for no reason other than my own unconscious modeling of my mother's behavior and my fear of her anger. I turned to him.

"French class was good, today, Dad."

His looked at me. His face brightened.

"Mr. Maiwald gave a really hard test but I don't think I missed any. I answered all the tricky questions and I wonder if that makes him happy or mad, but I'm guessing happy. I love learning French and someday I want to go and live in France."

"Oh, that's grand," Dad said. He loved the word grand. Or "Wouldn't that beat all," he liked to say, too, when something seemed unusual or special.

My mother seethed. I could feel her cold glare. There would be a price for this. She'd put me on restriction for a month for not making my bed or something else that didn't make sense. She didn't use the belt or yardstick any more, just her hands, to slap my face, and her harsh words, to sting deep. Too bad. I couldn't turn away from my dad any longer.

"We're learning about World War II in history class, Dad," I said, pushing my plate to one side. "You were in that Normandy Invasion, right? And all your stories, about the French people and the orphan Gilbert you wanted to adopt—that all happened when you were there, right?"

"Yes, that's right." He sat up straighter. We was over there in France for almost five months." Dad sometimes used "we was" when he got caught up in an emotional story. His parents, Scandinavian farmers who spoke with strong accents and not always the best English grammar, used that expression. I took a sip of milk.

"A lot of people died in that war, it sounds like. That must have been awful," I said.

"Yes, wars are always awful," he said and looked down. The frown line in this forehead deepened and when he ran his hands through his short, crew cut hair, I noticed how much it was graying around his temples.

Mom took out a cigarette from her packet of Winstons, which was always within reach, and tapped it onto the table. As Dad and I chatted more about French and what I was learning, he told his story again about how his French teacher's accent was so terrible that *merci beaucoup* came out sounding like "mercy buttercups." I always laughed when he talked about his French teacher, especially now that I was learning French. My mother's laugh sounded like a sneer.

"And with Gilbert—you spoke French with him, right?"

"Oh yes." Dad's eyes softened. It was as if he was watching a movie that only he could see. "Gilbert didn't know any English, though he learned a few words while we was there."

My mother had lit her cigarette. The smoke curled over her head and headed towards me. I heard her sharp inhale and the scrape of the metal legs of her chair against the linoleum as she stood up to leave. A moment later, the door to her room slammed behind her.

Dad sat drinking his coffee while I cleared the table and stacked the rest of the dishes in the sink. As I came back to wipe the table with the gray dishrag he started talking again.

"You know how you said you are learning about the Normandy invasion?"

"Yes," I said.

"Well I was assigned to go in on "D-Day plus one," as they called it, the day after D-Day. It was the luck of the draw. On June 6th, I was on a Navy ship just back from the coast. Those poor men who landed that morning, the Germans mowed them down."

His eyes looked glassy now and he spoke softly, almost to himself, looking down at his coffee mug. I slipped back into my sister's chair and leaned forward to listen, pushing the old dishrag aside. This was not at all like the other stories he'd told about his time in France.

"Something went wrong. The planes that flew over just before dawn missed their targets. So the men pouring out of the landing crafts, trying to run to the beach kept falling down, cut down by German bullets. It was a massacre."

He stared straight ahead now, not seeing me at all. He'd set down his coffee mug but was gripping it hard.

"Finally, one of the Navy destroyers, without orders—but the captain did the right thing for sure—pulled in close, firing over the heads of the men on the beach and blasting the cliffs. That and a few brave men, who made it up the hill and blew up the German bunkers, made it safer. But that was after hours and hours of slaughter."

He was holding onto his coffee mug so hard that his knuckles had turned white.

"I lost friends, other officers, and men I'd trained with and worked with for over a year, gone. Such a waste of human life in a few hours on that beach."

His eyes filled with tears.

"The next day, when I landed, the sea was red with the blood of all those young men, thousands of them dead. I'll never forget that scene on the beach."

Tears streamed down his face. I'd never seen my father cry. I reached over and touched his hand.

"Oh Dad, I am so sorry."

He looked up, startled. We sat in silence. He wiped the tears away with his white paper napkin and cleared his throat, trying to compose himself. His hand shook as he raised his coffee mug to take a sip.

I stared at the yellow Formica table and the old dishrag that had gathered up some crumbs and watched him out of the corner of my eye. This person, my father, who helped me with my math homework and handed out my three-dollar allowance each week, had seen so many things, far beyond the scope of what I could imagine. He'd been across the world, in two wars. What else didn't I know about him?

He passed something on to me that night, something unsaid about life and experience. He showed me how there are moments in each person's life after which nothing can ever be the same.

9

At the end of the following summer, I attended a five-day freshman orientation at U.C.L.A. called "Uni Prep." We stayed in dorms and took tours of the campus. Everyone chatted about which dorm they were going to be living in and seemed shocked when I told them that I was going to share an apartment with my sister and two other girls. The dorm sounded like much more fun, but the apartment, a cheaper option, had already been arranged.

At the end of the program, I took the bus from U.C.L.A. to Union Station and caught the train to travel back down south. My summer boyfriend Doug was going to meet me. I was seventeen.

At ten o'clock, when the train screeched to a stop in the dark, deserted station, Doug was waiting, just like he'd promised. I hugged him and felt relieved to have survived my first solitary adventure out in the world.

As we turned to go, I happened to glance down the tracks, and saw my dad, barely visible under the glow of a streetlight. He was there making sure I wasn't left alone at the train station at night. I waved, touched. He waved back, his typical high wave that resembled a salute just before he disappeared back into the shadows.

I didn't know that soon, my Dad would no longer be there, to make sure I was okay. At that moment, it was still a normal part of my life, something I almost took for granted. Almost.

A week later, I began at U.C.L.A., trying to find my way around the campus of thirty thousand students. Back in my hometown, population twenty thousand, where many of my kindergarten classmates and I had graduated from high school together, I felt stifled, but also secure in who I was, one of the "Johnson girls," an honor student, respected. U.C.L.A. felt cold and intimidating.

I had tested into French III and thought I could handle it. A much better idea would have been to go back to French II, to have a chance to get my feet under me and ease in. But I didn't ease in. It felt like I was dropped into the deep ocean and barely knew how to dog paddle.

We were reading *L'Étranger, The Stranger*, an Albert Camus text that, as far as I could figure out, was about a man who had murdered another man for no clear reason, was in prison and sentenced to death. The reading was confusing, depressing and I didn't even want to study it.

But the worst part was that my identity as the brilliant French student, the best in my school, sank fast. Excelling in French was how I knew I had a place in the world. I was so insecure and shy in every other way, but I did well in French.

But not at U.C.L.A. I cried a lot that first quarter and didn't study much. I earned a C in French III, my first ever grade in French that wasn't an A+. I never understood what happened to *L'Étranger*, sitting in his prison cell. I think they chopped off his head.

In high school, I had enjoyed writing and did well in English classes. But in my freshman English composition class, the teaching assistant wrote all over my papers with red ink and graded them as C-. Another piece of my self-confidence shot down, another area of failure. I decided then and there to avoid writing and to never take an English class again.

All the other freshmen were getting to know each other at the dorms, eating together, bumping into each other in the halls and forming little cliques that I couldn't find a way to break into. Being with Sharon helped, but I longed to feel more a part of college life.

Back at home, my parents separated and Dad moved into a trailer on the property. They didn't say anything about it, just acted like nothing was different. I didn't have the tools to speak up to them and ask what was going on, but felt confused and sad, which didn't help with my studies.

Winter quarter, again, the French was too hard and I felt swallowed up by the surging crowds of students flowing in and out of classes. By spring break, my mother had moved into an apartment and my parents had rented out the house. Life seemed upside down.

Even with this drastic change, my parents never sat us down and said, "Now look, this may be hard for you to understand but we're going our separate ways. It's not your fault, we just need different things and we still love you." Nothing was ever discussed. I was falling down deeper and deeper into a hole that I couldn't dig myself out of.

On that spring break, someone had the good idea that Sharon and I should have a formal photograph taken. I wanted to scream and she must have too, because the day of the photograph, we screamed at each other, then had to try to compose ourselves. I hated those photographs, a freeze frame image of "smile and pretend you're happy" in the midst of life caving in all around you.

Sharon and I had always gotten along well. But all of a sudden, I couldn't even count on my sister's love and support any more. Then spring quarter at U.C.L.A. again, French V, barely coping, getting B's and C's, getting by.

Since high school, I had dreamed of going to France my junior year for the study abroad program. A whole school year in France, to learn, to speak French and to travel. Many kids bought Eurail passes and traveled for the summer after, staying in youth hostels, having adventures, being kids. But the program required a B average in French classes and in general. I was not qualifying at this point.

By the time school let out for the summer, my mother had moved to an apartment in the classy beach town of La Jolla and was dating a scientist she had met in a bar. He seemed nice enough, had lots of money and offered Sharon and me jobs for the summer.

I was translating French scientific journals and Sharon worked in the lab. Most nights we went out to dinner with mom's beau to a restaurant named Bully's, where we dined on steak and he and Mom drank scotch on the rocks. My mother was on her best behavior.

Dad moved into a furnished studio apartment near his office in San Diego. We saw him sometimes on a Sunday, when he picked us up and took us out for the day. His apartment, where he ate TV dinners on a tray at night, smelled dusty and dank. He took us to Sea World one Sunday, which felt so awkward and formal. I just wanted my old life back, with my dad a normal part of it.

My mother's new life felt glamorous and fast-paced. My dad's felt lonely and painful. I didn't know how to help him and it all made me so sad. At eighteen, I found it so confusing that my loving and good father was suffering and my angry and selfish mother seemed to be thriving. I couldn't help being attracted more to her life than his, but my heart ached for my dad.

At the end of the summer, Dad announced that he'd accepted a promotion to be the Director of Design for the Pearl Harbor Navy Yard in Honolulu and was moving to Hawaii in September. At least he wasn't going to Vietnam, which had been one of his other choices. As a "dependent," I could go over with Dad, then they'd fly me back to start school again. I was so happy that he had found a way out of that dingy apartment and onto a new life.

I finished my summer job just in time to leave with Dad for Hawaii. I had three weeks before I began my second year at U.C.L.A. Hawaii! How amazing that I was going. I don't remember why Sharon wasn't going. The night before I left, my mother got drunk and turned on me. I watched her face, contorted and sneering as she sipped her scotch on the rocks, slurring her nasty words.

"He's just taking you because he doesn't have a wife to take—what do you think about that?"

She was trying to point at me, but could barely stand up and her finger wobbled and wove. Now I see what she was doing—trying to spoil my excitement and diminish Dad's good fortune. By then, I felt my own rage, confusion and sadness and her words felt like a punch in the stomach.

The next day, sitting on the plane, I let it sink in that I was off on an adventure with my dad. I had so missed him in my life. It didn't totally dawn on me that he was leaving California and going across the ocean to live; I didn't understand the significance of that then. All I knew was that I had three weeks ahead of me—just me and my dad.

Dad's office sent a hula girl to greet us at the plane with leis. The smell of the plumeria blossoms and the warm soft air felt new and fresh. The man who was retiring and whom Dad was replacing met us and took us to our hotel and out to dinner. It was a nice hotel, but, to my disappointment, not near the beach.

The next day, Dad left for work early and I decided to go to the beach. The only trouble was, Waikiki was miles away. But I put on my bathing suit and shorts and headed out in my tennis shoes, carrying a hotel towel tucked under my arm.

I walked along main streets with cars whizzing by for over three hours before I found a beach near Waikiki, set down my towel and jumped into the ocean. A Hawaiian girl about sixteen smiled at me and we struck up a conversation. She was staying with her ancient Hawaiian grandfather, who gave me a toothless grin. Throughout the afternoon, we swam and talked, and lay out in the sun.

She showed me how to get a frosty can of sweet guava juice out of the machine nearby and she and her grandfather shared some food with me. She told me that the beach was called *Sans Souci*, French for "without a care." *Great name*, I thought.

I also learned that there was a different language called Pidgin English that her grandpa spoke, which was why I couldn't understand most of what he said. Except "mo betta" which I could figure out meant "good."

They offered to give me a ride back to the hotel, a relief. The trouble was, the grandpa didn't want to leave the beach till it was almost dark. I knew that Dad would be worried, but I didn't have the number of the hotel to call. Finally, we got into the Grandpa's rusty, old blue Buick, rattled off, and found the hotel. Dad opened the door as soon as we knocked. He wasn't angry, just relieved.

"Oh Diane Mary, I was just about to call the police to go and look for you. I was worried sick."

We hugged and I apologized and he thanked the grandpa and my new friend. That night, we drove to Waikiki and found a hotel one block back from the beach, for the same price as the one his office had found for us. We moved there the next day.

From that point on, my days had a dreamlike quality. Dad left for work each morning early, I ate cereal in our hotel room and then headed for the beach. I'd see my friend or lie on the beach alone, read and swim. I explored the International Market Place, which was right next to the hotel. With all the walking and swimming and sun, I got tan, slimmer and stronger.

My mother was thousands of miles away and life felt so different without the undercurrent of her hostility. I was also out from under the shadow of my sister. In all my eighteen years, I'd never spent time alone in a new place. I discovered that I liked my own company.

My newfound freedom felt exhilarating. When Dad came home in the evening, we went out to dinner, trying new foods, like Hawaiian "hot plates" or Asian noodles with vegetables. Everything felt so exciting and different. We attended several welcoming parties for Dad in his new job and I noticed how everyone respected him. I felt proud of him.

One of my special memories of that time was one night at dinner. We sat in a booth enjoying some Hawaiian food and chatting about all the new and fun things we were discovering being there. Dad got quiet and I knew he wanted to say something.

"You know Diane Mary, I'm very excited about my new job and about being here. But I want you to know that of all the things that I have accomplished in my life, having a family has been the most important thing. Being a father has been the most important part of my life."

Hawaiian music played in the background and tourists in bright flowered shirts walked by in the restaurant. But at that moment, I felt like I was in a bubble with just my father and was very grateful. My dad was starting completely over, in a new place and life as a single man. But there was no question that first and foremost, he was my dad.

I helped him to find an apartment and to shop for things that he needed. When his VW bug arrived, we toured around to the other side of the island one Sunday, climbing the green hills and picnicking next to a waterfall. We jumped into the waves at beaches far from Waikiki. The hymn "How Great Thou Art" came onto the radio and he sang along, telling me that it had been his mother's favorite hymn.

In all my years of growing up, I had very few memories of time spent alone just with my dad. Once, when the family had gone to the Disney movie *Song of the South*, I was sick and missed out. When I was better, Dad wanted to take me by myself to see it and Mom said no. He took me anyway and mixed up with my mother's anger and disapproval was the thrill of how special it was to go to the movie with Dad.

We sat together in the almost empty Ritz Theater and during the sad or scary parts, I buried my head in his coat, feeling his warm and comforting presence. Those days in Hawaii with him had that same quality of connection, acceptance and love. I felt stronger and more confident in myself and got a glimpse of myself there.

I could feel my own feet under me as I breathed in the air full of the fragrance of plumeria blossoms. For those three weeks, life felt full of the promise of discovering this person called Diane Mary Johnson. Maybe my dreams were still possible after all.

I felt happy for Dad and his new life. But when I went back, what would I do without him, so far away? Just before I left, Dad wanted to buy me something special as a souvenir. I picked out a bathing suit and matching top which I had been admiring at the International Market Place, but unable to afford on my own. I cherished having that special gift to wear, to remember my dad and those weeks in Hawaii together.

Then it was time to say goodbye. Another young woman,

also headed back to the mainland to college, boarded with me. I walked up the outside stairs to the airplane and turned at the top to look back and wave at Dad.

He stood at the gate and waved back, then didn't budge while the plane taxied down the runway. I could see him out the small window, standing there, in his aloha shirt, all by himself. He got smaller and smaller, then the plane turned and I couldn't see him any more. I wiped away the tears and tried to clear the emotions out of my tight throat as my new friend chatted about college and boys.

I felt numb. Numb was how I'd functioned for eighteen years, how I'd survived the pain and chaos of living with my mother. But those three weeks had been so easy, so fun, so uncomplicated. I'd thawed out a little and felt the difference. To be numb again felt painful.

The night I got home, Mom was drinking heavily and made several cutting remarks about Dad. But the new and separate part of me I'd discovered in Hawaii just looked at her, almost with pity. I was on a high and at that moment, no one, not even my mother, was going to bring me down. But she gave it her best shot.

10

I was excited to move into a dormitory, like a *normal* college student. But I didn't realize that all the girls returning to the dorm after their freshman year had chosen a roommate. The one I was assigned, Sue, was the one no one else wanted and I soon discovered why. She was weird, hostile and liked to turn out all the lights and meditate to Ravi Shankar music and light incense when I was trying to study.

But on my side, Sharon hadn't organized a place to live. She ended up camping out with me on my narrow twin bed for two weeks until she found space in a sorority house that had extra beds. That was against the rules and Sue didn't turn us in. After Sharon left, Sue and I had a few rough times, but made a sort of peace with each other.

From my training with my mother, who was always upset with me, I assumed *everyone* was upset with me. But Sue was just upset, period, at her own parents, at life, not necessarily at me. She blasted Bob Dylan singing, "The Times They Are A-Changin'." I guess they were.

I loved my little space—one half of a narrow room, with a twin bed that folded back into a couch in the morning, a desk at one end and a closet with a mirror and drawers at the other end. It was my first experience of a space of my own, separate from my family, out in the world.

Living in the dorm gave me the freedom and the independence to come and go whenever I pleased. Everyone complained about the food, but I thought it was wonderful to show up and pick out what I wanted from so many choices, then just walk away from the clean up. As far back as I could remember, I'd been cooking, cleaning, and doing the dishes.

It was fun to make new friends and discover more about this person I'd caught a glimpse of in Hawaii, a strong, independent and happy eighteen-year-old. And right away, there was this cute, smart boy who really liked me and made me feel special and safe. He was going to medical school the next year and had a bright future. Mine was fuzzy, out of focus.

French was still challenging and I trembled at writing papers. My dream of doing my junior year abroad in France the next year felt out of reach. I didn't have the grade point average and if I could somehow get in, how would I pay for it? I had to work part-time jobs just to meet the expenses of college and wouldn't be able to work in France.

The excitement of my new life helped to distract me from those and other problems that I didn't want to think about. With my new friends, I could pretend to be an ordinary college student, just like them. But I missed my Dad—he was so far away. I never talked to him except on rare Sundays when we'd have a hurried phone conversation.

He wrote letters, at least once a month, when he sent me a hundred-dollar check to help with expenses. But I wasn't very good at writing back. What could I say? "I have a boyfriend. I'm not doing well in French—too far behind now to ever catch up." Everything I thought of saying would worry him, so I rarely wrote.

When my mother's relationship with the scientist ended, she drowned her sorrows in scotch and unleashed her anger at me—the same old pattern. I avoided spending time with her as much as possible. In the midst of all this turmoil, my boyfriend gave me a piece of that safe feeling I had lost when Dad moved away.

So when he pushed me to do things I'd never done as an innocent and "good Catholic girl," I gradually gave in. I felt reckless, with my parents divorced, my mother raging and my Dad living across the ocean.

By spring, I was pregnant. In 1968, to be pregnant before marriage, especially for a Catholic, was something to be ashamed of and hidden. All my mother's years of screaming, "You should be ashamed of yourself" rang in my ears. I was. My junior year in college I was going to be nineteen, married to a medical student, and having a baby.

My mother was furious with me and called my dad; I also wrote him a letter. His letter back to me began, "My dearest, darling daughter, Diane." He never once insinuated that I was bad or that he was ashamed of me. When we talked on the phone, I cried. I sat in my dorm room, at my desk by the window, looking out on the parking lot below, as I listened to his warm voice over the phone line.

"Everything is going to be all right now, so don't you worry. You take care of yourself and rest. And be sure to eat. How are you feeling?"

"Not so great," I told him.

"I'll come and help out before the wedding. Your new husband sounds like a good young man and he has a bright future. And by the way, what is your new name going to be?"

Dad arrived a week before the wedding. I hadn't seen him in nine months and his calm and loving presence felt so comforting. We had one week to pull the wedding together. Every day, we sat down and made a list.

Find a pillow for the ring bearer.
Go and buy the material to make the wedding veil.
Order the wedding cake

I was three months pregnant, had morning sickness and was tired. After our errands, we'd eat lunch out, such a treat, just Dad and me, like the days of the spam sandwiches. Then he'd insist I go and take a nap.

The day of the ceremony, I felt nervous and scared. How could I be getting married? My parents had just gotten divorced. I was supposed to go and live in France my junior year, not become a wife and mother.

Then Dad walked me down the aisle in my borrowed wedding dress. My mother wore a huge green hat. The old priest rushed through the ceremony. After a simple reception, some cake and good wishes, we rattled away in our 1965 VW bug that we'd bought for a thousand dollars, with a hand printed "Just Married" sign in the back window and cans dragging behind.

In those wedding photos, we are so young and innocent, nineteen and twenty, setting out into the world. We had no idea what we were facing. We didn't know that marriage is a piece of work, even under the best of circumstances, and that we had quite a few cards stacked against us—about to become parents, with limited money and nine years of medical school ahead of us, to name a few.

I didn't know that my parents' model of relationship would not provide me with the tools I needed to create a happy marriage. Or how much the unhealed pain with my mother would handicap me not only in my marriage, but in general.

I wanted to believe that it could all turn out, just like in the fairy tales, "happily ever after." I was young, I could do anything, I thought. And besides, it was such a relief to be moving five hundred miles away from my mother. I didn't know then that I would carry her harsh voice around inside my head.

At the end of the summer, we moved to San Francisco just before my husband Steve started medical school. On his first day, after a hurried bowl of cream of wheat, he rushed out. I wandered around the empty apartment, pulling my worn, pink, chenille bathrobe over my pregnant belly, trying to get my bearings and shivering, even with the hissing steam heater against the wall.

It had been one year since we'd met at a dorm dance at U.C.L.A. Now we were married and living in this strange city, where I knew exactly one person, my husband, who had just left, anxious and distracted about starting medical school. He'd been planning and waiting all his life for this day.

The breakfast bowls sat on the gray Formica table in the dining room, globs of cream of wheat stuck to them and to the pan, which was still on the stove. I was the one who had to clean this all up. That was my job now.

I missed my old life. I missed myself. I was just getting to know her, on that trip to Hawaii and in the dorm. But now I couldn't find her anywhere. I wanted to go back to bed and pull the covers over my head and cry. Some days in the weeks ahead, I did.

This was the first fall since I was four years old that I was not going off to school and it felt like the world was going on without me. At nineteen, I so didn't want to be left behind. My stomach grew larger by the minute and the new life inside me kicked and swirled around in her watery world.

How was I supposed to be a mother when I felt like such a kid myself? My mother had not been motherly to me at all. How would I know what to do?

My daughter came into the world, calm and peaceful, looking around with big, wide eyes. I held her in my arms and felt awe that my young body had created this perfect new life. We named her Michelle, inspired by the Beatles' song.

When I got up with her at night, I watched in wonder as she nursed, her tiny rosebud mouth moving till she dozed off, all warm and full. Then I snuggled her close, filling my senses with her sweet baby smell and soft skin before I tucked her back into her bassinette.

During the day, I could feel my father's love guiding me as I cared for my baby daughter, alone in the apartment. It felt like a lifeline, something good and pure, from his heart, to mine, to my daughter's and it kept me afloat, it kept me going. Who would my daughter grow up to be? What could she feel and know? I sensed that she felt and knew a lot.

My best friend Susan was doing her junior year abroad in Germany and I received postcards of her adventures in Europe in the mailbox in the lobby of our apartment building, on my way to the Laundromat.

I studied those postcards of some castle along a river or a famous city I remembered from a geography lesson. I thought about those places as I stared into the dryer and watched my pink cotton underwear spinning around with my husband's white jockey shorts, while a load of cloth diapers spun in the next dryer.

Then my baby daughter would gurgle and smile at me from her stroller and pull me back into real life, my life. Europe and France were a dream world of famous places and night trains through mysterious cities, with no Laundromats in sight.

But they were not my world. Those dreams had gotten buried, just like the overdue library books, under the stacks of clean cloth diapers.

Dad and I exchanged audiotapes and letters back and forth in the mail. His arrived with a monthly check of one hundred dollars, which paid our rent. The following June, Dad married a widow with four children, aged eight, ten, twelve and fourteen.

I felt happy that he was getting a second chance in life and love, but I knew that his marriage meant that he'd be staying in Hawaii for good. He'd been gone almost two years and was just so far away.

The Carpenters crooned their hit song, "We've Only Just Begun" on TV commercials, with images of happy couples on their wedding day, then starting out married life together. Getting married and having a baby seemed to be what happened in both old and modern fairy tales and then everyone lived happily ever after.

The only trouble was that our life was not a fairy tale. And neither my husband nor I had any tools to deal with real life, especially real married life, followed six months later by parenthood, at ages twenty and twenty-one, barely.

11

During my long hours alone, I noticed that I had two stations in my head. One was a quiet and calm station that loved the wonder of my baby girl and the challenges of motherhood and life, including how to figure out being newly married.

The other channel was broadcast from the twenty-year-old who wanted to be living in France, doing her junior year abroad and being a selfish, carefree, college student. I didn't know how to deal with my mixed feelings except to feel guilt. My Catholic upbringing made that easy.

My husband Steve, who had a full scholarship, studied hard. I took care of our daughter and did housesitting, baby-sitting and sewing for cash. I watched, amazed, as my daughter grew from a baby, into a toddler and then a preschooler who brought home finger paintings.

The world was changing fast too. San Francisco was the capital of "flower children" and hippie counter-culture and across the bridge in Berkeley, the university was erupting in anti-war demonstrations and riots.

The musical *Hair* shocked the world when the cast stood on the stage nude and the sexual revolution and women's liberation movement challenged all the rules. The use of birth control pills had become widespread. Abortion was about to become legal.

A friend from Berkeley invited me to join a women's "consciousness-raising" group that met once a month. Most of the women in the group were older, many were unmarried, and it provided a safe place for me to begin to unravel all my feelings about life, marriage and motherhood. I felt encouraged to begin to look for what I wanted and needed in my life, not just what society dictated.

I needed some help dealing with all the feelings that the group was unearthing and heard about a training hospital that offered counseling on a sliding scale. I qualified to pay a dollar per hour and signed up for twice a week, two fifty-minute sessions. I rushed to my appointments on the mornings that Michelle was in preschool.

The person assigned to me never said anything. I guess that was how he was being trained. But I felt so desperate to find some answers in my life that I went in there and talked for the whole fifty minutes, twice a week, hoping to unravel where I was bound up in my life.

I started to face some anger in myself. I began to see how my mother's behavior had contributed to my low self-esteem and how missing my dad after he moved to Hawaii had led to getting pregnant and married. I discovered longing. Longing for who I could have been, could have become, if I'd made different choices, if I'd seen my own value.

The Vietnam War was on the news each night. After giving birth and raising a child, I could see the insanity of war as a solution to any problems. I still had a difficult time expressing what I felt, but at least I was starting to know what it was.

I don't remember my mother much during those years when I was living in San Francisco, discovering mothering on my own. I was relieved to be so far away from her, buffered by a husband and a child. I was trying hard to be grown up, to play the roles I was in. Yet inside, I still felt like such a child myself.

Mom didn't write letters or call, so we rarely spoke or connected. She had started dying her hair red when she got a divorce. It was the era of mini-skirts and she wore a tight short, leather one, with high boots. Her chain smoking kept her thin.

She called herself a "single working girl" and her idea of who she was and the reality that she was in her late fifties didn't match. That's when I started to see how she lived in a fantasy world of her own creation and declared her world to be real, even though the two didn't match up at all. In my counseling, trying to sort out my feelings of doubt about myself and lack of self-worth, the path always led back to my mother.

My sister went to Europe to travel and then stayed on as an *au pair*, so my mother visited her several times. I heard tales of their escapades in Greece and Spain, always with some innuendos about Mom and various men. The sexual revolution was in full swing and my mother was swinging with it.

In contrast, my dad fit well into the role of husband again and stepfather. When I was being a mother and doing the things that mothers did, tucking Michelle in at night, reading her a story, comforting her when she had hurt herself, I could feel my Dad's love, pouring right back out through me. What would I have done without him in my own life and now, later, as I was navigating the waters of parenthood myself?

In spite of all the turmoil I felt with my own mother, I delighted in my sweet and smart little girl. My husband did too, and sharing that wonder helped us to stay together, even though we were both so young and mixed up in so many other ways. He was focused on becoming a doctor and didn't have time to question much else.

We lived in a one-bedroom apartment in married student housing, and as I met other young mothers, I never talked about what I was going through, trying to sort out who I was, with the world changing so fast around me. We also didn't talk about the stresses of being married to men who studied nights and weekends, were gone at the hospital and distracted and exhausted the rest of the time.

I heard whispers about one young mother who gassed herself and her baby in her parents' garage. They found her in time to save her, but not her baby. No one talked about how scary it was that someone who lived in student housing, in an apartment that looked exactly like ours, had gone over the edge. I don't remember talking much to my husband about it either.

We all just pretended it hadn't happened. It seems that the husband treated it that way too. He stayed with his wife, even though she had killed their child.

I grew up not talking about giant, troubling problems. But now things bothered me more. I may have talked about that with the counselor. I know I was deeply disturbed by it.

I continued the counseling, twice a week for two years. It did seem like I was sorting out some things and gaining some confidence, but since he never said anything, it was hard to tell. I talked a lot about my mother each session, trying to unravel all the different ways my relationship with her had caused me to feel so bad about myself.

Our last fall in San Francisco, the fall of 1971, my mom came for Thanksgiving. Sharon was back from Europe and living in San Francisco and we all got together at our tiny apartment for a turkey dinner. I was feeling good then, excited that the four years of medical school were almost behind us and enjoying my daughter, who was a delightful chatterbox of almost three.

During the dinner, Mom was exaggerating about something and I corrected her. She was furious with me for that, but I stood up for myself, telling her that she hadn't been telling the truth. We barely spoke to each other for the rest of her visit; luckily, she was staying with my sister.

My grandmother, Nana Daisy, died a few months later in early 1972 and Michelle and I flew down to San Diego for the funeral. My mother and her sister had argued when I was about eight and hadn't spoken to each other since. Surely they could bridge their differences and forgive each other as they shared the grief of losing their own mother?

But the hatred ran deep; at the funeral, they looked right through each other. I felt the sadness of watching that dysfunction and vowed that Sharon and I wouldn't end up like that.

The next day, my daughter and I were in the back seat of Mom's car and Sharon was in the front with Mom as we drove along. Out of the blue, Mom started raging at me, screaming and yelling, then slammed on the brakes, turned to the side and screamed, "Get out."

I sat there stunned. No one spoke, as the smoke from her cigarette curled up over her head and her words hung in the air. My sister Sharon stared straight ahead. Then my mother yelled again, this time turning her head so that I could see her face contorted in rage.

"Get out of the car." Her words came out like a hiss.

I didn't move. I could see the insanity of her leaving Michelle and me standing by the side of the road. I didn't get out of the car. Now when I look back at that scene, I see the pattern of my childhood—when my mother was in pain, she took it out on me. In this case, she was in the grief of losing her mother. But at the time, I couldn't see that.

I have relived that scene over and over and wondered, what if I had gotten out of the car? Where would we have gone? Would my sister have talked some sense into my mother to come back for us?

I would have had to knock on the door of a stranger's house and ask to use the phone. What would I have said? "My mother just kicked me and my daughter out of her car and could I please use your phone?" But I had no one to call. Everyone I could think of would have been a long distance call and I didn't have any numbers.

Maybe if I had been strong enough then, I could have gotten out of the car, walked away and never looked back. Maybe I could have stood up to her and said, "No, you can't treat me this way, especially with my daughter here. It is wrong, insane and unacceptable. Until you apologize, I will have nothing more to do with you."

But I didn't get out of the car. Michelle had to witness all of the pain being acted out in this very bad soap opera that I had tried to distance myself from. As we sat there in silence, she finally put the car into gear and drove off.

There were no apologies. Like so many painful moments with my mother, it would not be talked about again. But the pain of it was there, like a knife wound that healed over, but left a bright red scar.

Dad gave me his old Argus C3 camera with the hand-held exposure meter and I signed up for a photography class. Everyone else had fancy new automatic cameras with telephoto lenses, but I didn't care. I loved composing the black-and-white photos, then watching in the darkroom in wonder as my images emerged in the strong chemicals, onto the blank paper, as if by magic.

I wanted to emerge like that, to surface from blank to a clear image. But in my real life, it wasn't that easy. I'd had so many years of suppressing who I really was that when it came time to try to find me, I could only find the cardboard cut out I'd been, smiling and unmoving, frozen in time and cut off from her true feelings.

During that time, Carly Simon's hit song "That's The Way I've Always Heard It Should Be" contained the lyric:

I'll never learn to be just me first
By myself.

I listened to those words as I painted some wooden Christmas ornaments that I'd ordered from the Sears Catalog, my effort to explore painting. That's what happened to me, I thought, as I dabbed a blob of red paint onto a Santa suit. I never learned to be just me first, by myself. And I now have to weigh all my decisions of who I am based on whether or not they fit in with Steve and Michelle's lives. Who would I be, *just me first, by myself?*

I didn't know. But who I had been, before, by myself, had included French and France. Those passions had gone underground, with no outlet for three years. Then one day, in the laundry room near my apartment, I overheard a young woman speaking French to her tiny daughter. I listened with pleasure and smiled, but was too shy to talk to her. When I spotted her again a few days later, I told her that I'd studied French.

Claire and her husband were both radiologists, visiting from France to learn the latest medical techniques. I tried out my rusty French and we chatted, setting up a time to meet. She came over for tea with her two-year-old daughter, Hélène. Michelle said "C'mon Hélène, let's go!" and they ran off.

They were having so much fun that Claire asked if I would be willing to babysit so she'd be more free to participate in her training. I was happy to do that, so several mornings a week, Hélène came down to play with Michelle and I practiced my French. To Hélène, it was natural that I spoke her language and she loved playing with Michelle.

Claire and I took our daughters to the park on her free days. To my amazement, I still remembered a lot of French and still relished the way I felt when I spoke it or heard it. I couldn't explain it logically to Steve and he seemed to just tolerate this interest I had; a passion to know and speak French seemed so inferior to his life of becoming a doctor. But my dream woke up again.

Michelle turned three and it was time, the culture said, to have another baby. In fact, I was overdue. Most people had their children between two and three years apart. But I had just found my freedom again. I had some mornings to go to the darkroom or see my counselor, some time and space to myself, no more diapers and a little person to talk to and be with.

My husband was gone nights at the hospital and his internship, the year coming up, would be worse. The thought of staying at home with a new baby at that point did not make sense to me.

One of the young mothers who I had known in student housing had been so excited to move back to her home town for her husband's internship. She had a baby girl and a son who was two.

Six months into the internship, alone for days at a time with two small children, she took her life with an overdose of sleeping pills. The children were alone with her until the husband came home from his shift at the hospital—that could have been as much as two days. When they found them, the two-year-old had piled all his toys onto her lifeless body and the baby had screamed herself into exhaustion.

That was the second wife I'd seen crack. This time, she had died and not her child. But her children would be damaged for the rest of their lives after living through that trauma. Again, no one talked about this tragedy openly and I don't remember talking about it to my husband. But it influenced me at a deep level.

I decided that no matter what society thought was good for everyone else, I was not going to be home with a baby during my husband's internship. We were returning to Los Angeles and I was going back to U.C.L.A.

That summer, Dad and his wife Aileen stopped in for a visit on their way back from a trip to Europe, including some time in France. Dad had waited so long to go back to France; it had been almost thirty years since he was there in 1944. Unfortunately, his wife got sick on the trip, so they spent their time in Paris visiting doctors.

Dad and I were sitting at the kitchen table drinking coffee and chatting when he got quiet and I could tell that he wanted to tell me something. So I waited, looking out the window to the sweet peas I'd planted along a fence. Dad blew on his coffee, took a sip and set down his mug.

"Do you remember how I used to talk about the orphan, Gilbert Des Clos, who I tried to adopt and bring back to America?"

"Yes, I do remember your stories about Gilbert," I answered.

"Well, when we were in France, I was so hoping that we could get over to Normandy and I could look for him. We had one day free from the tour, so I had planned to take a train or a bus for the two-hour trip over to the coast. But then Aileen got sick and we had to spend that time seeing doctors." He stared down at his coffee mug and then looked straight ahead.

"I felt so frustrated. Here I was finally back in France, in Paris, wanting to get to Normandy to try to find Gilbert. Then I remembered that during the war, I'd been in Normandy, with Gilbert, wanting to get to Paris." He shook his head.

"Isn't life strange, sometimes?"

I nodded. He went on.

"So I thought, okay, I'll at least try to call him. I went into a phone booth and began to search through the names in the thick phone book. But I couldn't for the life of me remember how he spelled his name. Was it Du Clos or Des Clos?"

"I found some people with both last names, but then realized I was looking in the Paris book, not the Normandy one, and I'd never find the number there. I stepped out onto the sidewalk and stopped several people who were rushing by, hoping to get some help with my search. But when I tried to use my high-school French, the Parisians just shook their heads. I had to give up."

He was frowning, staring at his mug and sighed. I noticed the wrinkles around his eyes and how gray his hair had become since all those years ago when I'd sat with him, talking about Gilbert.

I hadn't thought about those stories from my childhood in a while, about France and the war and the orphan Gilbert. It was like they'd been put away with my childhood dolls and fairy tale books, a part of my life that was over but not entirely forgotten.

But I noted how it had been almost thirty years since Dad had been in France with Gilbert and yet he had not given up on finding him again.

"Dad, I am so sorry. That must have been frustrating. Too bad you couldn't have asked someone with the tour company to try to help you."

He looked up at me. "Oh, I didn't think of that. I should have done that. You're always so resourceful."

"Thanks Dad, I wish I could have helped you somehow." I patted his hand. "Maybe you'll get another chance to try to find him."

Dad nodded and looked at me.

"Yes, maybe so."

My father never traveled back to France for another attempt at finding Gilbert.

<h1 style="text-align:center">12</h1>

Back at U.C.L.A. that fall, I arranged my school schedule so that I took three classes, back to back on Tuesday and Thursday. I dropped Michelle off at her school at eight-thirty and picked her up at three-thirty, which gave me a few minutes at the end of the day to go to the library or the bookstore. My husband was on call every third night and working eighteen-hour days the rest of the time. When he did come home, he was exhausted.

In the four years since I'd left, U.C.L.A. had changed. Dorms were now coed, with girls and boys sharing floors and bathrooms. It was hard to imagine the strict visiting hours between boys and girls that had been in place, on Sunday afternoon from two to four, with the door left open.

I was now twenty-three, stronger within myself and extremely motivated about being back in school. I went to class, took notes and read all the assignments. Each night, after I tucked Michelle in, I studied till late. That first quarter, when all my grades came back as A's, I was thrilled.

I knew I was too far behind in French to major in it, so thought about Psychology. But the huge classes, about lab experiments—rats and mazes and at best, monkeys—graded by multiple-choice exams, felt unsatisfying.

In contrast, I tried out a Cultural Anthropology class. The intimate classes and interesting and challenging subject matter felt refreshing. They were finally asking the deep questions I was interested in, what is a human being, beyond the imprint of culture? Who are we, really? I chose Anthropology as my major and got to work.

But my struggles in my freshman English composition class came back to haunt me. Now, as a junior, and a Cultural Anthropology major, I had to write papers. What was I to do? I was terrified of failure again. By chance, I heard of a place on campus called The Learning Skills Center and shyly walked in. A nice man sat me down and listened as I burst into tears and poured out my story that I couldn't write and was sure of failure and could he help me?

He handed me the Kleenex box and waited as I tried to compose myself. Yes, he could help me and why didn't we start right then? I left that day with another appointment and a few tips to approach writing my next paper. When I went back with my first efforts, he encouraged me with kind words, pointing out the places where I had been able to put down some clear thoughts. We worked to organize those thoughts and I left again with more of a sense of what to do next.

Over the weeks, I worked on my papers late into the night. Winter quarter, in the Psychology of Women class, the readings were powerful and stirring. The class reminded me of my consciousness-raising group in San Francisco.

We read the book *Our Bodies, Ourselves* and many other texts that told the stories of women all over the world who where trying to find their identities and power within cultures that barely allowed them a voice.

I relished the small discussion groups led by teaching assistants who were more my age, though none of them had children. I discovered that, faced with a blank piece of paper and an assignment, I had a lot to say on these subjects, a lot more to say than the single coeds sitting next to me in the class. I got an A in the class but more importantly, I found that writing helped me to discover what I knew and thought and gave me a way to express it.

The class also stirred up a lot of feelings within me about the role of motherhood. I had never questioned that I carried the burden of raising and taking care of Michelle, while my husband was free to pursue his career. In the class I read about other cultures where there was no distinction between the word for "mother" or "aunt" and children ran free from one hut to another, looked after by the whole village.

Where is my village? I wondered, as I went through my days alone with Michelle. How is it that in our culture, we have isolated ourselves and especially women, home alone with children? It just didn't make sense. Luckily, I made friends with two other mothers and we helped each other out a lot.

But still, every night, I was at home alone with my one child. Steve wasn't that interested when I tried to talk to him about all I was learning and would usually fall asleep as soon as he got home. But I was looking and learning, thinking and writing and so grateful to be back in school.

I found a counseling center on campus and started seeing a woman named Mrs. Katz, who was motherly, encouraging and kind, such a contrast to my own mother. She helped me to see and to acknowledge my strengths and my courage—to return to school, married, with a preschooler and a husband who was gone most of the time. With my continued success in school, I began to feel more confident and stronger within myself.

My life took on a balanced rhythm of being a mother, a student and, once in a while, a wife. I continued to get straight A's and was moving forward again in the direction of my own dreams, toward a goal, and discovering myself along the way.

It was as if I came into focus again, in my own vision. I discovered a passion for learning, a strong intelligence waiting to be used and, of all things, a love of writing.

The contrast between being a student two to three days a week, studying at night, and excelling at U.C.L.A., and being a mother and watching the growth and development of my little girl the other days, felt wondrous. When I took a child development class, I'd experienced all the developmental stages they described first hand.

I loved all the reading, especially all of Margaret Mead's books on sex and temperament in primitive societies. The idea of Mead tromping around through New Guinea and Samoa in the 1930's, exotic and foreign places I had to look up on the map, inspired me. A role model, at last. Steve was mostly gone, but I felt so fulfilled within myself that I didn't resent his absence.

Because I was on the Dean's List, I could petition to take graduate classes offered through the Department of Psychiatry in conjunction with the Anthropology department. In one class, there were twenty students and three professors, some psychologists, some anthropologists. The professors were not that much older than I was and had young children too, so I felt a rapport with them.

During class, we engaged in deep discussions about what we were reading and studying and the professors listened and seemed interested in our thoughts and ideas.

We had assignments that took us out into real life, into our culture, observing and writing down what we discovered, rather than just discussing theories from books. In one small class of about thirty with a world-renowned professor, our assignment was to keep a journal of all the rules of our society and all the "rule violations" that we saw during the ten weeks.

"What rules?" we asked, at the first class.

"Just wait," he said. "Keep looking and writing about what you notice."

So I watched and listened and wrote about my life as a student and a young mother. The professor was right. After a few weeks, I started noticing rules and their violations everywhere and had plenty to say. There were all the rules that my daughter and her friends were trying to learn, sometimes succeeding better than others. When she and her friend Jill had to be reminded, more than once, to not play doctor, that was a rule violation.

When I noticed that I was attracted to the young gymnast who ran my gymnastics class, that was a rule violation. I was twenty-five and married. I was not supposed to think thoughts like that.

I worked on my paper at night after I tucked Michelle into bed. She liked to listen to Disney records on her record player as she fell asleep, the soundtracks of *Alice in Wonderland* and *Robin Hood* being two of her favorites.

As soon as I kissed her goodnight, I sat down at my standard Royal typewriter, which I had found at a yard sale, at my tiny desk by the window in the dining room. The Disney songs played in the background and, after a while, the scratching of the needle at the end of the record, told me that it was time to turn it off.

I tiptoed back into her room, touching my daughter's soft cheek as she slept, clutching her worn and much loved brown teddy bear, then hurried back to the desk. I typed and pondered, my fingers finding the keystrokes that led to the words and then the sentences that gave a voice to the person I was discovering. A warning bell chimed when I had five letters left before I had to hit the carriage return to start the next line. Who was this woman who wrote page after page about our society, rules, life, marriage and motherhood?

I had two sheets of "easy erase" paper in the typewriter, with a carbon in between. I often made mistakes, typing not being one of my strong suits. Erasing them meant rolling the papers out, carefully correcting both pages, then winding it through and spacing in to where I had been on the page. If I was lucky, it all lined up.

I felt pulled like a magnet to putting words on paper, formulating thoughts into sentences, distilling clarity out of confusion. Finally, someone was asking the questions I'd wanted answers for since I first started school. And the professor wanted to know what I thought, felt and discovered about those questions. How grand.

I wrote over two hundred pages in the ten-week quarter. The professor told me that my paper ranked as one of the best he had ever received in all of his years of teaching, and had I considered graduate school? The A I received was great. But the real gift was to hear my voice, to tap into my depth, my clarity, humor and even audacity.

I liked her. There was no turning back now.

The summer before I completed my classes at U.C.L.A., I received a President's Undergraduate Fellowship to create a project and carry it out. I designed one in Hawaii, studying cultural differences in preschoolers, and Michelle and I flew over to stay with Dad and his family for six weeks. It was so lovely to have such a long visit with Dad. I hadn't spent more than a week or two with him since he moved there.

I wanted to complete my degree before having a second child, and with just one quarter left in the fall, was happy to be newly pregnant. Staying with Dad and his family also gave me some help with Michelle so that I could take naps. The project went well and Steve came to visit for a week in the middle.

I completed my classes at U.C.L.A. in December 1974,

six months pregnant; I planned to go through the graduation ceremony the following June. Just weeks after the birth of my daughter Heather in April, we bought a fixer-upper house.

The house had a nice feel, a fireplace and thick stucco walls with archways between the rooms. But years of neglect had left it dirty and unkempt, with bare mattresses on the floor, carpets that smelled like cat pee and an overgrown yard full of weeds and trash.

Somehow in those first few weeks, we tore up the old carpet in the bedrooms and cleaned and waxed the lovely oak floors that were hidden underneath. We painted the two bedrooms with rollers while Heather slept in another room in her baby seat and Michelle helped out by painting a closet. Then we packed up and moved into the new place.

I was not resting nor easing into the changes in our life with a newborn. There was just so much to do. Dad kept calling to find out how things were going and though I tried to minimize it, it still sounded like too much.

Then he called and announced that he was taking his retirement early so that he could come and help out for a month with the new house. That was the best news I'd heard in a long time. When Dad arrived, we made a list of things that needed doing, prioritizing it.

"Now everyday, I want you to take a rest," he insisted.

No problem, I thought. He fixed the clogged plumbing, buying two huge red pipe wrenches, saying they were a gift to us for our new home. Over twenty years later, alone on my property with a broken water pipe gushing like a fountain, I'd dig out those old wrenches and bless him.

He painted, plastered, and cleaned, working steadily every day, just stopping for lunch and dinner. I marveled at his skills and so appreciated his kind spirit there with us. His presence was so comforting. I did rest many afternoons and felt my strength coming back. Michelle liked having him there to talk to and be with. Steve was grateful for how Dad took care of so many things that needed doing.

One day, when Heather was sleeping, I dashed out to run an errand. When I pulled up to the house, Dad was out on the front porch, holding a wailing bundle in a blanket and crooning in a loud voice, "Ya, ya, ya, ya." That must have been what his mother did with his younger siblings. I'd never seen Dad hold a baby before. It was so cute, but he was clearly panicked, watching and waiting for me to come back.

When his month was over and he had to head home, I cried. What would I do without him? The house was so empty, the yard still filled with weeds and so much left to do, though we'd made huge progress.

The person I had become, the strengths I'd discovered by returning to U.C.L.A., writing two-hundred-page papers and graduating with honors, started to recede into diapers, dishes and loneliness.

I'd been so free for almost three years. Now I was tied down again, at home alone in a house with a dark kitchen and so much work crying out to be done. I had a six-year-old who was having a hard time adjusting to sharing her world with a new baby and a husband who was still rarely home. Some days I felt like I was sinking and couldn't find my way up to the surface.

During that time, I took a weekend extension class at U.C.L.A. called "At a Journal Workshop, the Ira Progoff Method." In the workshop, we dialogued with people from our lives, with our bodies, even with events and things. It felt so nourishing to have some time for myself for the hours of the workshop; I ran home during breaks to nurse Heather.

Something opened up in me that weekend. I wrote and wrote, the words flowing out like a dam had burst open. The power of the writing stunned me. We had the opportunity to read what we'd written out loud and I raised my hand. When I tried to read, I had to pause many times as I choked up with emotion I hadn't known was there.

The woman psychologist who led the class offered an ongoing weekly group nearby so I signed up and began going. All of the unresolved feelings I had from getting pregnant, married and becoming a mother at twenty were resurfacing now that I was home again with a baby. Unresolved anger at my mother and continued problems with her showed up often in my deep journaling. Little by little, I felt some space opening up around me and narrow shafts of light coming in.

During that time, I took another workshop where we were supposed to pick words that represented deep traits that we wanted to express in life. I chose "fiercely independent." I was so far from living those words right then, completely dependent, nursing a new baby, but something inside of me wanted to be that, which both shocked and excited me.

Who was that person who wanted to be fiercely independent, and where was she buried?

13

My husband's nine years of medical training and our time in Los Angeles were almost complete. I wanted to move back to Northern California to a small town, either in the mountains or on the coast. I found Nevada City in books on small towns in California and we went for a weekend to check it out. I thought it was charming, but he thought it was too small and too cold, so that was that.

I also liked Santa Cruz, a town on the coast, south of San Francisco. But he had made up his mind that he wanted to move to a town north of L.A. and start a practice. I was excited to be getting out of L.A., but felt angry that I hadn't had more say in our decision of where to live.

Just before we left L.A., I attended an evening French conversation class held in a woman's home, once a week for six weeks. We sipped French wine, nibbled hors d'oeuvres and chatted in French.

I looked forward to that two-hour class all week, relishing the sound of French again, struggling sometimes to recall words and phrases, but remembering a lot and understanding most of what was said. It was my two hours a week to dress up and feel like my old self again, with something precious of my own.

A part of me woke up in that class. I was high for hours and even days afterwards, hearing French echoing in my brain as I hung wet diapers out on the line, did a sink full of dirty dishes or read a bedtime story. French became my private world again where all things were possible and the problems of normal life didn't exist. In that world, the sense of "me first, by myself" felt like a lifeline and I held on tight.

One of the first things I did when we settled into our new town was to sign up for more French classes at the community college. My husband was still gone most of the time and my life, with a two-year-old and an eight-year-old, was busy and full.

But those hours in the French class felt so fun and fulfilling and fueled me for all the shopping, errands and busyness that filled the rest of my life. I became friends with the French teacher and my daughters and I spent time with her and her two sons, who were bilingual.

I also read every book I could find on personal growth. One of the books talked about Erhard Seminars Training, known as "the est training," which claimed that you could change your life in two weekends. What a concept.

In my own work with counselors, it seemed like it took years to make even the smallest changes. I was twenty-nine and getting impatient to free myself from the pain that haunted me. I could gamble two weekends on the chance that it worked.

The first day of the training, I was riveted. Thank God! Here was one of the rare places where they were talking about the real things in life, the questions and answers I'd been searching for. It was like they'd gone out and gathered up two hundred people at random——college professors and waitresses, truck drivers and musicians.

And yet, each person who shared and interacted with the trainer said something I could relate to. At the end of the two weekends, I felt lighter and freer about my mother and life in general.

I also completed two journalism classes, hoping to find a way to channel my love of writing into a job out in the world. The teacher encouraged me and even told me about a part-time opening at *The Ojai Valley News*, a small newspaper near my home.

Feeling more bold and courageous after completing the est training, I applied for the job. For my interview, the publisher and I sat in a booth at the local coffee shop, while he read over my resume and scrutinized me over the top of his glasses.

"I see here that you studied Cultural Anthropology and French at U.C.L.A."

"Yes, I did." I waited.

"Newspapers report on American culture. And if you know French, you know English grammar. Your background is perfect. You're hired."

I let out the deep breath that I didn't know I'd been holding and had to smile for all the times I'd heard, "You'll never get a job with those majors." I started the following Monday, scrambling to arrange childcare, my biggest hurdle.

For my first assignment, I interviewed the Peace Pilgrim as she walked through the town. The petite, silver-haired seventy-year-old had been walking for twenty-five years for peace and would walk for three more, covering over twenty-five thousand miles. After the interview, I went back to my desk and sat down at my antique Royal typewriter to write up the story, which was due that afternoon.

As I faced the blank, white paper wound into the typewriter, all my doubts came up to haunt me: Who do you think you are, pretending to be a writer? You've only taken two journalism classes! You'll never be able to do this. They're going to find out that you're no good, that you're a fake.

Such hateful and harsh thoughts. The job was shining a spotlight on the general sense of unworthiness that I'd worn like a cloak around me for most of my life. But then an amazing thing happened. Because of what I'd learned in est, I saw and heard those thoughts clearly and knew that I had a choice whether or not to listen to them. I took a deep breath, sat up straight and began to type up my story. It ran on the front page of the next edition and the publisher was pleased. I was ecstatic.

I loved the balance of the days at home with my daughters contrasted with the three days a week working at the newspaper. There, I was a separate person, using my mind and abilities out in the world doing something that I loved—and getting paid for it.

I breathed in the smell of the printing presses when I walked in each morning. In those days, the term "cut and paste" referred to the real process of cutting out stories and ads and pasting them where they needed to go before printing.

I relished the adventure of not knowing what story I'd be assigned and then jumping in and doing it, forming the thoughts, polishing them and then seeing them in print a few days later. It felt so powerful to say "I'm with the newspaper" and gain access to otherwise closed worlds. The temporary position lasted six weeks. I'd replaced a woman who was out on sick leave and she was coming back. But I had tasted the joy of being a writer.

For the next year, I took more classes with est and developed a group of close friends. In our open and authentic relationships, we talked about real challenges in our lives, without pretense. I also developed an identity and friends separate from my family and my marriage. Life went on as before, but I felt different inside of it. I had some tools to begin to sort it out.

My husband didn't share my interest in personal growth or est. I was still looking for the answers to the important questions from my childhood, but he wasn't asking those questions and he didn't seem interested in ever asking them.

This had probably always been true, but during this time, the freer I felt, the more our differences stood out. Our arguments and difficulties made me feel like I was reliving my parents' marriage, which filled me with panic and dread.

After I did a course with est called the "Six-Day Course," everything changed and came into focus. In it, we had to jump off a mountain on a zip line, rappel down a steep cliff and pull ourselves across a canyon, among other challenging things. I signed up for the course because I was terrified of heights and still quite scared of life in general, especially that people would find out that I wasn't good enough.

During the six days, I discovered that everyone thought that they weren't good enough, everyone had some kind of pain that they were trying to overcome and I wasn't the only one with negative voices in my head. I also discovered that I could be terrified of something and go ahead anyway.

The second that I stepped off the mountain on the zip line, I screamed out in joy, swinging my legs and arms and pulsing with energy and excitement. I left the course with a new sense of what was possible for me in my life.

The man who created the course and led it, Landon Carter, also impressed me. He was well educated, classy and handsome and yet had dedicated his life to trying to discover how to be free and to helping others to move beyond their minds' limitations.

He had an authenticity and directness that felt refreshing and rare. I thought he was the most amazing man I'd ever come across. He was married and I was married, but I tucked his image away as my ideal man.

He had just changed my life in ways I could only begin to imagine. The experience of those six days would stay with me as I journeyed forward, knowing that I could bring fear along with me, rather than letting it stop me. I could hear my mind screaming, but listen for the calm, quiet space.

That would make all the difference.

Turning thirty made me take a long, hard look at my life. I could see that if I didn't, another ten years would go by, or twenty and I'd still be where I was—unhappy. My husband and I had been married eleven years and were stuck in painful patterns of arguing. I suggested to him that maybe if we separated for a while, we could find a way to work things out. I envisioned us possibly starting fresh with some new tools. My husband agreed to the separation, but within a few days, got together with a woman from work and didn't look back.

That shock buckled my knees, bringing up my worst fears of not being good enough and a tremendous feeling of abandonment. My marriage was not that strong to begin with or he could not have walked away, but I didn't know that then and went through a lot of pain.

Luckily, my new friends helped me through. I called one woman at two in the morning, feeling like I couldn't make it through one more minute of that sleepless night. She was so kind and comforting, telling me that it would be all right and that one day, I would look back and remember how strong I'd been. She was right, of course. I was so much stronger than I knew.

But being divorced presented big challenges. The pain from my mother showed up in my relationship with my oldest daughter, who blamed me for the divorce. All those sweet years when she was my little buddy in my early twenties got lost in her teenage anger. How had I created this? And how could I deal with it?

My husband wanted joint custody when we divorced. We had argued for years that he wasn't home enough, didn't participate enough with the family and with the kids and now he wanted joint custody? Okay.

So I ended up, as a single mother, with time alone for the first time since having my daughters. Whole weekends of time stretched out ahead of me and I had to deal with my own loneliness and terror of being alone.

I needed to start earning money, a challenge with two young daughters. I managed to find a niche in sales and marketing, which became a stepping-stone out into the world and helped me to build some confidence. Having flexible hours allowed me to work around my daughters' schedules.

The job at the newspaper had been temporary and didn't pay enough, so I had to let go of the dream of being a writer, at least for a while. I kept up my journal writing and promised myself that someday, I would find a way to go back to writing again as my job.

Three years later, I was dating a man named Roger who realized how much France meant to me and thought it would be great fun to go. Dad had old-fashioned values and I knew he wouldn't approve of me traveling for a month with someone I was dating. So when I told him about my trip to France, I was a bit vague and I didn't talk to him much about it.

I look back now and wonder why I didn't think about his stories of Gilbert or about helping him to try to find him on my trip. But those stories from my childhood were buried far back in my life at that moment, when I was trying to navigate being divorced, working, relationships and a new life.

I arranged for day camps for my daughters and my husband agreed to cover the nights. I put the airplane tickets on an American Express Card that I could pay off over time. I had the time now, but not a lot of money. Later, I might have more money, but not a lot of time. I needed to go.

I'd studied French off and on for nineteen years, without ever setting foot in the country. It was like I'd been rehearsing to play a part and finally was stepping out onto the stage. As I reviewed French and worked with a tutor to prepare for the trip, I could feel that old magic and excitement coming back into my life.

Would the fantasy world I'd created as a teenager and held onto for so long fall apart when I finally fulfilled the dream? I couldn't wait to find out.

14

The moment I came up from the R.E.R. (*Réseau Express Régional*) train into the street in Paris, all I could do was stare. It felt like I'd stepped into the pictures I had seen all those years ago, with Sharon and Holly in the French I book—the sidewalk *cafés*, crammed with people chatting in French, sipping café out of tiny cups, smoking those long French cigarettes. Waiters scurried about, tiny French cars honked on the busy streets and people rushed past. I stood with Roger and blinked and smiled.

I loved the challenge of speaking French and found us a hotel, for five dollars a night, in the Latin Quarter, near the Sorbonne. The shower down the hall delivered only a spindly stream of hot water, but our room had a tiny balcony with French doors. I was transfixed.

We found our way around the city to see the sights, the Eiffel Tower, the Arc de Triomphe, Notre Dame Cathedral, and the tiny chapel of Sainte-Chapelle. I did well with the French, ordering meals and navigating the metro. There was just one major snafu when Roger ordered a "hamburger." When the meal arrived, a piece of bright, red, raw hamburger meat with a fried egg on top decorated the plate.

Roger, being from the Midwest, was appalled that the meat

was raw. The waiter, being French, was appalled that Roger was appalled. I tried to calm things down as well as I could. We sent it back and it came back *bien cuit*, well done, though the waiter did throw the plate down in front of Roger. Ah well, one rude Parisian waiter wasn't so bad.

We rented a car to tour across France and into Germany and Switzerland. Roger wanted to visit Germany and had some friends in Geneva. Once across the border into Germany, I felt uncomfortable, not being able to speak the language. At one point, we were lost and stopped to ask directions at a gas station, but were unable to communicate with the owners at all, even with lots of sign language and gesturing.

As I turned to leave, I noticed a John Wayne movie dubbed in German on their television. At that moment, something snapped inside of me—John Wayne speaking German? That was the last straw. I convinced Roger to head back to France.

Days later, as we drove through the Rhone Alps in France, just over the border from Switzerland, we passed Lake Annecy. We only had one afternoon to swim in the sparkling, clear lake, but I vowed that some day, I would come back and spend more time.

We were going to visit my friend Claire, who I'd met in San Francisco; she and I had kept in touch for ten years with Christmas cards. From Annecy, we took the winding mountain road towards Nice, passing miles and miles of meadows bright with wild flowers.

Late in the day, needing to find a place to stay, we stopped in a tiny village. At the edge of the town square, a rusty "Hotel" sign hung crooked off its hinges. The brown letters were so faded, I could barely make out the sign, *Hotel de la Place*, Hotel on the Square, one star.

As I entered the lobby to ask about a room, the high ceilings and worn, but elegant furniture made me feel like I'd stepped back in time. I rang the bell on the desk, and an older woman came forward, dusting flour off her hands onto her white apron, her gray hair pulled up in a bun. She seemed a little hesitant, guessing that I was American, but smiled and looked relieved when I spoke to her in French.

Yes, they had a room and it included dinner and breakfast. They grew their own vegetables, raised their own chickens and baked their own tarts, which she had just been doing. *Formidable*. What a find. I booked the quite inexpensive room and went back out to tell Roger.

Upstairs, in our large, spacious room, right along one wall, stood a modern shower stall; it must have been a recent upgrade. Lace curtains fluttered at the windows, which looked out over the extensive garden and farmyard out back. *La Toilette*, the toilet, was across the hall.

That evening, downstairs in the dining room, tall candles flickered on the tables, which were covered with starched, white damask tablecloths and napkins. Our dinner included five simple and tasty courses. A rich "potage" or vegetable soup, fresh green salad, roast chicken and vegetables, a cheese tray and an apple tart with thick cream, all served with a local Côtes du Rhône white wine.

The owner's daughter, who served us, told me that the roast chicken we were enjoying had been clucking around the yard earlier in the day. The meal had a quality of freshness and flavor both delicious and nourishing. We felt like honored guests as they served us course after course.

As I conversed in French, I felt softer and less certain than in English, but there was the connection, the smile of recognition, the moment of bridging what could have been a gap, because we could all understand the same sounds.

In that tiny village, in the hills above Nice, where we were the only Americans, we'd dropped into the old world of

France. That one night stands out as such a vibrant memory and confirmed what I already knew—speaking French in the real France was even better than I could have ever imagined.

The next morning, in the sunlit dining room, we feasted on fresh croissants, baguettes, butter, jam and coffee and the family bid us goodbye as we set off for the coast. After a fun visit with Claire and her family, we poked our way across France in our tiny rental car, enjoying the little beach towns along the Mediterranean and the open fields of lavender and sunflowers.

A few days in Paris at the end, and it was time to go home. But I carried within me the wonder of the trip and was already dreaming of how to return. Back at home, however, the reality of my life, however, as a single mother and making my way in the world, meant that thoughts of future visits to France had to go underground again. I listened to French songs, treasured a French *Vogue* magazine and went to French films, just to have a taste of the language and the culture that so fed my soul.

I couldn't explain it logically—why was I so fascinated with a place so far away? It was so much more practical to learn and know Spanish, with Mexico just a few miles south of where I lived. But I'd given up long ago trying to solve that mystery. I adored French and now had a real experience of the country. I would find a way to go back.

My daughters and I managed to visit Dad in Hawaii a few times and he came to California, so we saw him about once a year. I still found my relationship with my mother challenging and frustrating, but had become resigned to it. I trained to become a life coach and found the work not only helped others, but contributed to me too.

That career choice allowed me to have a flexible schedule to accommodate my daughters and it also fit with my desire to continue my search for the real answers in life. I was learning the tools of communication and the importance of following your dreams. The work also helped me resolve some of the challenges with my teenaged daughter.

Roger and I split up but stayed friends when it became apparent that he wanted to have children and I didn't; I was just beginning to have some space again with both my daughters in school. I dated, but enjoyed my freedom too much to even consider marriage. I was discovering that "fiercely independent" woman who had called out to me all those years before, and I liked her.

During the summer of 1986, I had a stretch of six days with no kids and an airline voucher for a free flight. My dad's birthday was July 20th, so I called him and asked if he'd like a very special birthday present—a visit from me! He was thrilled. I hadn't been back to Hawaii in three years and it was such a joy to relax and spend time with Dad.

At the end of my stay, he took me to the airport, and as always, walked me right up to the gate. Dad liked to be early. "Better an hour early than a minute late," he always said, so we had plenty of time before my flight boarded. We found a coffee shop near the gate, with gray Formica tables between brown vinyl covered seats, and sat down.

Dad ordered coffee and his favorite dessert, a piece of apple pie. When his coffee came, he tapped his sugar packet on the table, first one side, then the other, before he put it into his coffee. I'd seen him do that so many times and wasn't sure why he did it, but it made me smile, it was so "Dad."

I drank tea and we chatted about the visit and how great it had been. As he ate his pie, I told him about my work as a life coach and how much I enjoyed feeling like I was helping people in their lives. He nodded and listened attentively. But there was something I had wanted to say to him for a long time and I sensed that this was the chance.

"Dad, do you remember when I had pneumonia when I was eight and was in the hospital?"

"Of course I do. You were so sick and if it hadn't been for that experimental drug and that new young doctor who was willing to try it, we could have lost you." He frowned and shook his head.

"Well I had an experience there that I always thought was just a dream, but since then, I've read about it a few times. It is called an "out-of-body experience" and is what happens to some people when they are dying and leaving." He nodded, put down his coffee mug and leaned forward.

"That night, you were there, sitting in a metal chair, dozing off, and all of a sudden, I could see you from up above. I was no longer inside my body, but looking down on the whole scene, including me in the bed and you in the chair. Then, I could feel myself floating away through the wall towards a golden glow and I felt so free.

"I was headed towards that glowing light, right through the wall and that is when I woke up to the fact that something must be really wrong—I couldn't move through a wall! I looked back and saw you again, sitting there in the metal chair.

And in that moment, I knew that I was leaving, that I was dying, and that if I let that warm glow pull me out through the wall, I would never come back."

I took his hand across the table.

"I knew that you would be so sad, that it would break your heart. I could feel your love for me and it turned me around and pulled me back into the room. Thank you for being the one who demanded that they do something to save me and for being such a loving presence in my life that I wanted to come back—I couldn't leave."

By that point, we were both crying, holding hands across

the gray Formica table in the coffee shop, as travelers bustled all around us, rushing to catch their flights. The waitress hurried by, her rubber-soled shoes squeaking on the linoleum floor, coffee pot poised, ready to lean in to refill Dad's coffee, then glanced at us and kept moving.

I grabbed some paper napkins from the metal dispenser next to the catsup and handed a few to Dad. We wiped our eyes and blew our noses, both unable to speak for a few moments.

Thirty years had passed since I'd been lying in that hospital bed, but sitting there in the airport coffee shop, beyond all of the years in between, all of the confusion of my mother's anger, my parents' divorce and the failure of my own marriage, I could feel how my father's love back then, and now, was real and precious in my life.

It felt so good to thank him for who he'd been and was for me. I had a lot of uncertainty in my life, but knew that I could count on Dad's love. I was so blessed and deeply grateful. We both composed ourselves and sipped some water to calm down.

"Thank you, Diane Mary, for telling me that. I do remember those days in the hospital, and how your life seemed to be hanging by a thread. I'm so grateful that you did come back."

"Me too, Dad."

They called my flight and we gathered up our things, walked to the gate and hugged goodbye. I boarded the plane and could see him standing there, waving, even after everyone else had left. As the plane taxied down the runway, he got smaller and smaller, standing there in his Aloha shirt, till I couldn't see him anymore.

My relationship with my mother hadn't improved over the years. She still dyed her hair red, wore tight clothes, smoked and drank, liked to party and stay out late. She was now in her seventies. She had gone through lots of different relationships and didn't seem interested in my daughters, her grandchildren. She criticized my life choices, not understanding why I wanted to be a life coach and didn't get a "real job" doing something important.

I didn't see her much and when I did, she often lashed out in rage, as she always had, even on one occasion, blaming me for her divorce. It felt sad to me that Dad was the parent who lived so far away and she was the one who lived closer.

Part IV

1989

15

My dad turned seventy-five in the summer of 1989 and three generations gathered in California for a special weekend. We celebrated his life, told stories and took a group photo with Dad and his wife in the center of all the kids and grandkids. I noticed that Dad seemed thinner and I was concerned, but he said that everything was all right. I so wanted to believe him.

I will always remember the moment when I knew that everything was *not* all right with Dad. It was early 1990, a few months after Dad's big birthday party and I was sitting at my desk, looking out the window overlooking my back yard, the same view I'd looked at so many times before, as we chatted on the phone. He said something about going to the doctor and I immediately picked up on it.

"What's wrong Dad?"

"I'm having some tests," he said.

"What kind of tests?" I could feel a sense of panic as my voice rose in pitch.

"I've been having some weird symptoms and they're trying to figure out what is going on, that's all."

He'd been experiencing some problems with his vision and a few other unexplained things. I made him promise that he'd let me know as soon as he found out anything more. He promised. A week later when I called him back, he didn't want to tell me—he was afraid I'd be worried. But I was already worried. I just wanted to know the truth.

He had a rare form of cancer called Waldenström's. I listened in shock as he told how he was going to go through chemotherapy and that they were hopeful that he'd be all right. He had good doctors, he reassured me.

I got off the phone and sat still, staring out the window. My father, who had never taken a sick day in his thirty-five years of working, could not possibly have cancer. His parents had lived to be eighty-five, his grandparents even longer. This could not be happening.

I walked around my house and thought about him over in Hawaii, facing cancer and chemotherapy. I longed to be able to go and see him, but couldn't see how to take time off from my busy life. But what if we didn't have much time left?

I called Dad every few days to see how he was doing. He tried to minimize it, but the chemotherapy was making him really sick and he was having blood transfusions. After a few months of hearing about his suffering, I made a decision. I would take a leave in my practice as a life coach, move out of my house, put my things into storage and go and spend time with Dad. As soon as I made that choice, I felt a huge sense of relief. It took two months to tie up my life, stuff all my worldly belongings into a storage unit and head to Hawaii.

I spent a month with Dad, helping to take him swimming to Sans Souci beach where we'd gone together through the years. He was weak, but the warm ocean water seemed to relax him. I read him books. I recorded the stories about his childhood, growing up on a farm during the Great Depression.

All those years ago, he interviewed us with a wire recorder. Now, I was interviewing him with a tape recorder. He talked again about his time in the war in France, in 1944.

His frail body regained some of its youthful vigor as if somehow tapping into the strong, young man who turned thirty while stationed in Normandy, a lieutenant junior grade who became a full lieutenant by the end of the war. He was tired and nauseated from the chemotherapy and losing his eyesight, but his eyes shone as he talked about his part in the invasion that stopped Hitler's occupation of Europe.

He'd loved his time in the Seabees, building the artificial harbor, the Rhino Ferries, the camp above Omaha Beach, and repairing bridges in nearby towns. I saw then how his job during the war had been to restore and rebuild things, amid the destruction and devastation.

He was reliving the most powerful time in his life and I realized then how much I had never heard before. He'd always been so attentive and supportive in my life, but how much had I paid attention to his? There was so much about my father that I didn't know. He spoke again about Gilbert Des Clos. He still said Gilbert's name with a soft G sound, the way the French said it.

"I wonder whatever happened to him," he said, and he became quiet and seemed sad. I patted his fragile hand, wishing there was something I could do. I didn't want to push him and wear him out, so stopped our taping for that day.

By the time that I left, after a relaxed four-week visit, Dad seemed so much stronger and we all hoped that he would be all right. During that month, realizing that I could lose Dad, I examined my own life and values and decided to leave Southern California, with its hectic and expensive lifestyle. So when I flew back, I packed up a carload of things and drove north to stay with my sister Sharon and her family.

Sharon's family lived in Nevada City, the same small town in the foothills of the Sierras that I wanted to move to years before. I loved the quiet and peace of the mountains, the clean, fresh air, dark night skies and the comfort of being near Sharon. After a few months, I rented a studio nearby.

Over the years since our parents' divorce, Sharon and I sorted out our relationship and healed the problems that had surfaced, beginning when Mom and Dad separated. We figured out that we had taken sides in the divorce and were fighting their battles.

Our bond was strong and good again, even though Sharon was closer to Mom than I was and clearly her favorite. Somehow, like in our childhood, we navigated those stormy waters and helped each other to face the pain and trauma of Dad's cancer.

I worked with my coaching clients long distance and began developing new clients locally. Because of my simple lifestyle and low rent, I slowed down and relaxed a bit, a relief after years of hustling to keep up an expensive lifestyle.

That winter, I couldn't explain why, but I felt drawn to renew my efforts to learn French. I invested in a video series put out by Yale and began again. As I worked with the videos, I was surprised by how much I remembered and how much I understood. I listened and watched in my little studio while cooking, sewing or doing other projects.

I kept in touch with Dad by phone, but could tell that he was struggling so in March, went back to Hawaii to see him. When I had left the summer before, he looked strong and well, more like his old self. But when I saw him again, it was shocking to see how much he had declined in just eight months. I knew then that Dad was losing his battle with cancer. When my mother heard that Dad was failing, her comment was, "Tell Donald he should have caroused more." Dad reacted to her words with a wincing smile.

I had to accept the painful reality that it was just a matter of time before I lost my beloved father. I couldn't imagine life without him, but I also hated to see him suffering like he was. He'd lost so much weight and was losing his eyesight. He didn't complain, but it was so hard.

We talked about what he believed about life after death. I read him a poem by Mary E. Frye that said it well:

> Do not stand at my grave and weep
> I am not there. I do not sleep.
> I am a thousand winds that blow.
> I am the diamond glints on snow.
> I am the sunlight on ripened grain.
> I am the gentle autumn rain.
>
> When you awaken in the morning's hush
> I am the swift uplifting rush
> Of quiet birds in circled flight.
> I am the soft stars that shine at night.
>
> Do not stand at my grave and cry;
> I am not there. I did not die.

After I read him the poem, he became very quiet.

"Dad, do you believe that you have a soul that will live on after your body dies?" I asked.

"I'm not sure about that," he responded.

"Well, I believe, like in the poem, that after death, your soul will still be alive, just not in your body."

"Well, that's a comforting thought," he said.

While I was there, I helped to take Dad swimming a few times. It was a challenge to get him in and out of a wheelchair and in and out of a special warm pool. He was so thin, that he got cold really fast, but he seemed to enjoy moving in the water, so it was worth the effort.

I had written a poem for Dad, thanking him for being there for me when I was a child. Now he was living the last days of his life. One day, I was sitting outside with him, watching over him while he walked a few paces back and forth in front of the house.

He stopped and looked at me and I looked up.

"Diane, you know that poem that you wrote?" I nodded.

"That was real nice."

He looked over at me, smiled, then kept shuffling along, holding onto the walls to steady himself as he went. I wiped away a few tears while his back was turned, touched that my poem had meant something to him and that he'd told me.

At the end of my six-week visit, when I said goodbye to Dad, the thought of not seeing him again made me determined to return as soon as I could. I did not want this to be our last goodbye. For the first time, when I left Honolulu, Dad was not standing at the airport gate and waving. I began to feel the loss of him, piece by piece.

The Ways of the Heart
A poem written for Dad
January 6th, 1991

Time seems to change things, Dad...
I remember...
When I was small, you held my hand
as we crossed the street
you steadied my way and guided me, protected me
while my little legs grew strong and true

We'd stop and rest
I couldn't keep up with your strong long legs

Now I hold your hand as we cross the street
I steady your way
I guide and protect you
Your legs
have grown weak
We stop and rest
you can't keep up with my strong long legs

Thank you, Dad for the gifts you gave me
for showing me love
for teaching me so well
and allowing me to share it back with you

bodies grow and change
but hearts remember love and
there is no time in
the ways of the heart

16

In the background of my life, always present in my thoughts, I knew my father was fighting for his life. When I talked to him on the phone, his voice had lost its rich timbre; he whispered now. But it was still Dad. He was still there, barely, but still there. I booked my flight to go back.

Summer turned to fall, the days got shorter and the leaves started to turn and float down on the light breeze. Fall represented a time of death, when nature let go and surrendered to the quiet of winter, then burst out again in the spring.

But this autumn, I knew that I would lose my father. What would I do without him? He'd always been there, a light in my sometimes dark life, loving and encouraging. He and Sharon had been my anchors. I understood then that I had moved closer to Sharon at this time of losing Dad so that we could help each other through our loss.

My flight was delayed and I arrived late in the evening, but when I walked into the hospital room, Dad was sitting up, eyes open, present and alert. Even though he couldn't see me, he knew I was there the moment I walked in—he looked right where I was in the doorway.

I hugged his frail body and then sat down holding his hands. He couldn't see the tears flowing down my cheeks as we talked.

It was so good to see him alive. He asked about the flight, the family. We had a good visit. He's doing all right, I thought.

His wife Aileen and I got him settled down for the night. I left and went back to their home, the familiar place I'd visited so many times since Dad had married Aileen, twenty-two years before. The bathroom smelled like Dial soap, with stacks of *Reader's Digest* in the magazine rack and worn towels hanging from the wooden towel racks. I settled into my room and slept, tired from the long journey.

The next morning, I returned to the hospital and when I walked in, he was sleeping. I sat with him and waited for him to wake up so that we could visit. But as the hours passed, he didn't wake up; he'd slipped into a state of semi-consciousness.

As I sat by his bed and watched him, I realized he'd waited for me to arrive so that we could have a real visit—one last conversation. We would never have another conversation like that, like we'd had thousands of times before.

Once or twice that day, he woke up and looked at me for a moment, seemed to be there, then slipped away again. I tried to wake him and to help him to eat when the food came, tried to get him to at least take a sip through a straw of the canned, thick, chocolate drink they brought to feed his skeletal frame. But he didn't have the energy to rally.

The hospital buzzed outside his room, elevator bells chimed, meal and medicine carts rolled down the polished hallways. Once in a while, a nurse came in to check on him for a few moments. They left him alone, as if they couldn't face that he was dying. But that was just not right.

On the third day, I called in a male nurse and asked him when was the last time they'd changed his bedding, his gown or bathed him? He didn't answer me. And couldn't they please turn him so that he didn't get bedsores? After my insistence, the nurse checked Dad in a perfunctory way. I had to say something.

"He was a pilot, you know. Learned after World War II on the GI bill. He so loved to fly. And an engineer with the Navy, here at Pearl Harbor and in World War II."

The nurse paused, looked up at me and then at Dad. I could see the moment when Dad became a real person for him, not the thin, almost lifeless form lying on the bed. How I wish now we could have taken Dad home. But I didn't know then about hospice.

By the fourth day, I was angry at what felt like their neglect of him. I would take care of him if they wouldn't. I told them I wanted to bathe him, to please bring me all that I needed, dry shampoo, warm water, towels and cloths. And then I wanted a clean gown and sheets for him afterwards.

They brought it all. He was deeply somewhere else by then, only waking up for brief moments and then not knowing where he was, who he was or who I was.

I washed his emaciated body with the warm towels, drying him right off and covering him to make sure that he didn't get cold. Because he was so thin, I could see how huge his frame was, his giant kneecaps, hands and feet, his large head.

As I bathed him, I was reminded of taking care of my two babies when they were tiny. I knew back then, that it mattered that I was gentle and loving, because there was a soul inside that couldn't respond back yet, but that soul knew and felt my love. That day, washing my father's dying body, I knew that he, too, could feel my love, just like my babies had.

I held my hand up to his. I'm not tiny by any measure, but my hand was only half the size of his. He'd always occupied a huge space in my life and now I could see that physically he *was* huge. When they turned him so that I could wash his back, I winced at the bright red bedsore on his lower back.

I washed his hair with dry shampoo, shaved him gently, to make sure I didn't cut his face, then splashed on his favorite aftershave, Aqua Velva, which he'd worn my whole life. It was so Dad, that smell. I brushed his teeth and combed his clean hair, then called them in to change his sheet and gown.

My father had gotten up each day at five forty-five, showered and shaved, splashed on the Aqua Velva, brushed his teeth and was ready for the day. I had never once seen him unclean or unshaven.

He visibly relaxed as he settled back into the fresh sheets, wearing the clean gown, his body now clean. Lunch came and again he couldn't wake up to eat. I felt so many emotions—anguish at seeing him like that, sadness, and distress. I held his hand, closed my eyes and prayed.

Dad's uneaten lunch sat on the tray beside him. Shiny red Jell-O, orange- green pureed vegetables, overcooked chicken and another can of the thick chocolate drink. The smell of it made me nauseous. I pushed it away and took his huge hands in mine.

Dad, I said, talking directly to him, psychically. *Dad, I can't stand to see you like this one more minute. You've fought with great courage, but the cancer has won. Please don't hang on for me or for Aileen, trying to protect us from the pain of losing you. The pain of watching you suffer is more difficult. It's okay for you to let go now.*

I'm here till Tuesday. If you let go today, I can call everyone and they'll be able to come. I can organize the memorial services—I can do it all. If you wait, Aileen will have to face it alone and that would be hard for her.

I know that you worry about me, that I'm alone. But I'm strong, Dad. I'll be all right.

You are so precious to me—you taught me how to love by your love. I will miss you and always remember your love and your goodness, but I don't want to remember you like this. You can go now, Dad.

It was early Thursday afternoon. I knew he understood what I'd sent to him with my thoughts. I cried as I sat with him all that afternoon, holding his hand and stroking his face. How mysterious life is, I thought. He'd sat next to my hospital bed, when I was eight, to keep me here. Now I was sitting next to his hospital bed, to help him to let go. The nurses didn't come in. He didn't wake up for dinner.

I left about ten when Aileen came to sleep in the room with him. She'd been doing that for a few nights since he'd been waking up disoriented and frightened, unable to see and not knowing where he was. She'd comfort him and he'd go back to sleep.

The jarring jangle of the old dial telephone woke me up at three in the morning. I had to stumble to another room to answer it, but knew what it was before I picked up the receiver.

"Your dad is gone," Aileen said through the phone line.

"Oh, okay, I'll be right there."

I ran to the bathroom to splash cold water on my face, when the reality hit me. He's *gone.* Oh no. I turned to the towel rack next to the sink to dry my face when I felt a jolt of energy hit me in the chest.

Pow. He was letting me know that he was okay.

Wow, thanks Dad. That helps.

Though I couldn't prove to anyone that I'd felt that jolt, I'd felt it. And I knew it was *him.* It lightened the heaviness in my heart.

I made the familiar drive to the hospital, through the deserted streets of Honolulu, parked, ran through the doors, up the elevator to the fifth floor, down the hall past the nurses' station, to the room on the left.

But the bed was empty. They'd already taken him away to the morgue in the basement. They needed the bed for another patient. Just his hearing aid and a few personal items sat on the side table for us to take home.

"Tell me what happened," I said to Aileen. I wanted to know.

"He woke up and was disoriented so I got up to comfort him. I wanted to sing to him, but the only song that came to mind was one that he taught me from his time in England during the war, before France."

"So I started in on *I've got sixpence, jolly, jolly, sixpence, I've got sixpence, to last me all my life...* It seemed to calm him down and I felt better singing it. When I got to the last line, *and we go rolling, rolling home*, he chimed in the last words *dead drunk.*"

"Then he settled down again and I went back to the cot to sleep. It was a while later when the nurse woke me and told me that he had passed."

It was sweet to imagine the scene of Aileen singing to Dad and Dad chiming in the words to a song he'd sung during such a powerful time in his life. I had to smile at the irony, that though my father had never been drunk in his life, his last words had been *dead drunk.*

He had felt the words that I had poured out from my heart the afternoon before. He had let go. I was so glad that he had slipped away in his sleep, with his wife right there beside him. I kept my word to him and called everyone to come and arranged for two memorial services, one at his church and a military memorial at the Punchbowl Cemetery where his ashes would be interred.

The next challenging task was to write his obituary. I scanned the newspaper to get a sense of what to write. I read one for an eight-year-old girl who had just died, another for a forty-year-old man, then one for a woman in her fifties.

I realized that at seventy-seven, Dad had had a full life.

He'd traveled the world, successfully raised four children and four stepchildren, served in two wars and had a busy and active life right up until he got sick. When I finally wrote the words *"Donald Kenneth Johnson, 1914-1991,"* I felt a sense of peace.

Sharon asked to see Dad's body one last time, to be able to say goodbye. Even though this was not what they had planned, Aileen agreed. But that also meant that we had to pick out some clothes for them to dress Dad in. Aileen and I chose his favorite Aloha shirt, a pair of pants, a belt, underwear, socks and shoes. One of their friends offered to drive the clothes over to the funeral home.

"Tell them to be sure to not tuck in his shirt," I said. That one detail was so important, for the last time that we'd see him in those clothes. Otherwise, it just wouldn't be Dad.

"Okay, I will be sure to do that," the friend agreed.

Early Saturday morning, Sharon, Aileen, her youngest son and I went over to the funeral home and sat in the room with Dad's body. He looked like he was sleeping, there in his Aloha shirt that wasn't tucked in.

I was grateful that I'd bathed him on Thursday so that he had been comfortable in his body on what was to be the last day of his life. We sat in silence and said goodbye to the physical form of the man who had been such a large and loving presence in our lives. As we left to go back to the house, it began to rain.

"In the Hawaiian culture, rain is considered a blessing," Aileen said.

"That's good," I said. The idea of a blessing at that moment felt right.

Later that morning, at the memorial service at Dad's church, the space overflowed with family and friends who came to pay their respects. Dad had been a volunteer with the Coast Guard

Auxiliary and a large contingent of his group came in uniform. Dad would have loved that.

We sang "Amazing Grace" and "How Great Thou Art," his mother's favorite hymn, the one he and I had listened to on the car radio, driving around the island together when I was eighteen. One of Dad's friends from the church read the poem that I had written for Dad, "The Ways of the Heart." People came back to the house after the service, bringing food and comfort and trying to help us to fill the void.

The following Monday, we gathered again at the Punchbowl Military cemetery. In the ceremony, the solemnity of the taps and the crack of the guns in the twenty-one-gun salute gave a finality to Dad's life and reminded us of his service to his country. They presented a flag to my brother, as the oldest son.

After the ceremony, as we stood around, I looked at the urn of ashes with *Donald Kenneth Johnson* inscribed on it and the tears started to fall. How could my father be in that little box? Right at that moment I felt another jolt of energy and heard Dad's voice, loud and clear, almost shouting in my head, *"Do not stand at my grave and weep, I am not there, I do not sleep."* The words startled me and made me remember the poem I had read to Dad.

Okay, Dad. I forgot for a second there. Thanks for the reminder.

That second sense of him "on the other side" letting me know that he was okay lifted the grief and sadness. In the photographs from that day, large white spots appear around my brother as he is holding the flag, just the moment when I started to cry.

Some people say those represent the unseen spirits, their energy caught on the film. I had heard him distinctly, right then, when the photo was taken.

Back at the house, going through Dad's things, Aileen

showed me a file from his desk where he kept all my communications with him through the years. For every phone conversation, he jotted down notes. Every letter I wrote was also filed, in order. There was so much love in that file. I held it close to my heart, then added it to my pile of things to take home.

Tuesday morning I had some time before my flight back to California. I went down to *Sans Souci* beach, that special place I'd discovered at age eighteen and where I'd gone with Dad and our families in the twenty-four years since.

All of my senses felt heightened—the sky seemed bluer, the palm trees greener as they swayed along the shore. The ocean felt cool and refreshing on my skin, as I moved through the water, feeling my strong legs propelling me along.

I'm alive and healthy. Life is such a gift. Thank you, Dad, for showing me that. You're gone now, but I will never forget your love.

I knew that I was still in a state of shock, and that the loss would sink in as time went on. But those moments felt like a gift and a balm as I prepared to leave Hawaii and to begin life without my father.

17

Back in Nevada City, I retreated to my cozy studio in the chilly fall weather, relishing the simple ritual of lighting the wood stove for warmth and making soups for dinner. Many times I picked up the phone to call Dad before remembering, *Oh that's right. He's gone. I can't talk to him any more.* Being close to my sister and her family and spending time with my daughters helped me to deal with the emptiness.

I also felt soothed by the quiet presence of nature all around me. The huge pines that touched the sky, the stars that twinkled through the tree branches like Christmas lights at night and the subtle changes of the seasons, day by day and week by week.

It was as if nature hit me over the head each time that I walked out of my door and said, *wake up, look around, be present, here, now.* I relaxed into that space and relished the wonder I witnessed each day. After the quiet of a snowy winter, the apple trees at the farm just up the hill burst into fragrant white and pink blossoms, reminding me of the gift of new life that spring represents.

Life felt rich, living more simply, in my tiny, handmade studio, just down the hill from the beautiful apple farm and a short walk from my sister's house. My rent was so low, that I could slow down a bit and still put aside money, looking forward to the day when I could return to France. I had not been back to France since that first trip in 1982, but could feel the mysterious pull and the longing to go again.

For two years after my dad's death, I watched my French videos, soaking my brain with the melodious sounds and learning new words and phrases. I still had a practice as a life coach and wrote a lot in my journal, but hoped to find a way to become a writer again.

In 1993, I took a class at the community college on how to be a successful freelance writer and the teacher kept emphasizing the importance of writing about what we were passionate about. When I realized that the 50th anniversary of D-Day was coming up the following June, I decided to write an essay telling how growing up with Dad's stories about the war and France had influenced my life.

And what if I could somehow journey back to Normandy, to remember and to honor Dad? With both of my daughters in college, I could arrange the time to go. When a friend offered me his air miles to make the journey, I knew it was the chance I'd been waiting for. I booked my flight.

A few weeks later, after taking the train from Paris to the shiny, modern train station in Rennes, I sat alone on a bench waiting for my connection to Bayeux. A kind man asked me where I was headed and when I showed him my ticket, he pointed out a train a few tracks over—I was sitting in the wrong place. I ran and jumped on the vintage, red train just at the last moment before the conductor blew the whistle.

We chugged along through the Normandy countryside, passing apple trees laden with bright red fruit and hefty black and white cows munching the fall grass. I left my empty compartment to stand in the aisle and lowered the large metal window to let in the fresh October air.

I was forty-four years old. I had been studying French for thirty years, with just one trip to France. But on this trip, my second, I was fulfilling my dream of traveling alone on the train, finding my way, speaking the luscious sounds to buy baguettes, cheese and fruit and to find a hotel.

I felt the significance of traveling back to the Normandy coast where my father had spent over four months during the war and excited to write an essay in his honor for the 50th anniversary of the D-Day invasion. I hugged myself in a glow of happiness and satisfaction as I stood at the window, felt the cool breeze and watched the landscape change as the train chugged and hooted along its way west.

At the family-run, one-star hotel in the village of Bayeux, where I'd reserved a room, the young woman at reception welcomed me warmly. When I mentioned that I was researching an article about the D-Day invasion in honor of my father, she told me that a group of English World War II veterans were also staying in the hotel and encouraged me to meet them that evening when they gathered.

I carried my bag up the narrow wooden stairs to my third-floor room, which looked out over rooftops and across to the cathedral. The tiny room consisted of a double bed, covered by a worn but clean comforter, an antique dresser with a white embroidered doily on top and a sink, with clean white towels. The *toilette* and shower were down the hall. *Perfect.*

That afternoon I wandered and explored the town, visiting the cathedral and the famous Bayeux tapestry. The quaint village had escaped extensive bombing during the war and the Norman buildings and winding streets retained their old-world charm.

The next day, I was scheduled to take an intense, all-day tour of the D-Day Invasion beaches, so I enjoyed my leisure time. At lunch, I sat in the sun at an outdoor café near a rushing creek and enjoyed a salad and a glass of white wine, relishing the joy of living in French in this corner of France.

That evening, as I came into the hotel again after dinner, the receptionist told me that the English veterans, gathered in a room off the lobby, wanted me to join them. When I walked into the room, about thirty elderly men sat at tables, chatting. They were in their late sixties and seventies, many of them wearing their brown, belted uniforms from the war, some covered in medals.

Their caps, jaunty wool berets, and a few officer-style hats, sat on the tables. Their hair was white and their faces wrinkled, but they became animated, their eyes twinkling, as they laughed and kidded each other and told stories of their time together in France all those years before.

They were enjoying their dessert course, an apple tart, and insisted on ordering one for me. Large carafes of wine and a few bottles of whisky and Calvados circulated among the tables. They welcomed me like a long-lost daughter and I felt honored to be included in their gathering. As I told them about Dad's part in the war, they listened and nodded their heads.

One very frail man stood up to speak, wobbling as he leaned on his cane, his voice coming out just above a whisper. Another younger man jumped up to stand by his side, to help him if needed. The frail man had a lot of medals on his uniform and everyone leaned forward to listen to his words with respect. They were remembering the glory that they had shared in being a part of such a major event in history.

As the evening went on, when they mentioned members of their group who had died, either in the invasion or since, many of them wiped away tears. Their frailness and sweetness reminded me so much of my dad that I also became teary. Had Dad's battalion gotten together like this too, I wondered? If so, he had never talked about it. They gave me hugs, pats and many hand squeezes before I said goodnight, wishing me well with the tour and with my story.

The next day, I wiped away tears as I stood on the cliffs above Omaha Beach, where my father had stood almost fifty years earlier, before I was born. The all-day tour taught me so much about the invasion that turned the tide of World War II and began the defeat of Adolf Hitler. Knowing the whole story also created a new context or backdrop for my father's stories.

Now I was there after my father's death, retracing his steps and remembering him, his stories and his love. It all felt poignant and important, as if something inside of me was saying, *pay attention now, slow down and listen.*

On June 6th, 1994, the 50th anniversary of the invasion, my essay, "Touching the Heart of D-Day" appeared in several newspapers. It described my journey back to Normandy and how Dad's stories about his time in France had colored my childhood, especially the one about his relationship with Gilbert Des Clos. I was thrilled to have sold a freelance essay about a topic that meant so much to me and to restart my writing career.

The TV was full of specials about World War II, with powerful images of young soldiers landing on the beaches, laden down with packs and guns, running and dodging the rat-a-tat of German bullets. I watched all the specials, adding to the knowledge I'd gained on my tour the previous fall.

Thousands of veterans, now in their late sixties and seventies, were traveling back to France, many of them for the first time since the war, to remember and to honor their fellow soldiers who had died and never returned home. The touching ceremonies at the American cemetery above Omaha Beach felt especially moving, reminding me of my powerful visit.

When my youngest daughter Heather was fourteen and started studying French, we made a deal that if she continued with her studies of the language, then, when she was nineteen, we'd travel to France together for a month.

I thought Heather might change her mind between fourteen and nineteen, and want to travel with her friends—the backpack, Eurail pass, youth-hostel trip. But at nineteen, she still wanted to take the trip with me. I was excited that I was returning to France so soon, on the long awaited trip with Heather.

Because of my success with the D-Day essay, I set up other articles to write, about traveling with Heather and about French seawater therapy spas, which I'd read were healing and wonderful. When Heather was home on breaks from college, we watched French videos together, knowing we were practicing for our upcoming journey.

During the busy weeks before the trip, something told me to send a copy of my D-Day article to the French Consulate in San Francisco. They had someone there called a press attaché who might be interested. So I followed that hunch, and wrote a quick note attached to the article, saying that I was returning to France in a few weeks and would be taking part in the 50th anniversary celebrations that continued throughout the month of June.

A few days later, the press attaché from the Consulate called and invited me to meet with her before I left for France. I'd never been to the French Consulate or spoken with a press attaché. So I agreed and drove the two-and-a-half hour trip to the city for the meeting.

At the Consulate, I felt as though I had dropped into a tiny island of France and relished hearing French spoken all around me. The press attaché welcomed me into her elegant office and thanked me for the heartfelt article. She nodded and smiled as we chatted about my upcoming trip with my daughter. Then she leaned forward and spoke with great intensity.

"Madame Covington, while you are in Normandy, you must try to find the orphan Gilbert Des Clos."

I paused, touched by her interest in the story, but not sure how I could do what she asked. I'd thought about looking for Gilbert on this trip; I'd had the conversation in my head, over and over: Was it possible? How would I look for him? Could I find him, would he even remember?

"But I don't know how to even begin to find him," I replied. "And it's been fifty years!"

"I know, but you don't understand. The French don't move around like 'les Américains'. He will still be right there, in Normandy," she insisted.

"Here is what you do. You place a *petite annonce*, a little ad in the newspaper in Normandy. It's called *Ouest France*."

She turned to the side of her desk and looked up the address and phone number of the newspaper on her Minitel computer-like device, wrote it on a slip of paper and handed it to me. I put it into my wallet where I knew I wouldn't lose it. As I stood up to leave, she took my hand and held it as she spoke.

"Madame Covington, promise me you will try to find the orphan Gilbert. Promise me you will place the ad."

I paused and looked back at her, quieting my busy mind, full of pre-trip preparations, for just that moment.

"I promise," I said.

18

I was excited about the chance that I might find Gilbert Des Clos, even though it seemed like a remote possibility. But I was mainly focused on the trip ahead with Heather. I was thrilled that I was taking her when she was nineteen, the age when I had so wanted to go.

I worked for months creating a full itinerary for us, from Normandy to Nice and back again. It had been twelve years since I visited Claire and her family, but we planned to visit them in Nice.

Just before our trip, I stayed up late one night, typing out our itinerary with all the phone numbers for my sister. Something told me to include the fax numbers listed at each place, even though neither Sharon nor I had a fax. I couldn't have explained why to anyone, but I felt compelled to put those numbers in there.

I listed every appointment I had, even places we were just stopping for lunch, where I had a meeting with a local person to gather information for one of my articles. I couldn't think why Sharon might need to try and reach us, but I put all those details on the itinerary.

I handed the neatly typed pages over to Sharon just before I left, in a red file folder labeled in bold black letters: "Diane and Heather's itinerary for France trip, 1994." Sharon put it on the counter next to her phone in her kitchen. In her busy life as the mother of three, she would be able to find it there.

Heather and I flew to Paris and spent a few days discovering the "City of Light" together. We toured the Louvre, sipped cafés in sidewalk bistros, visited Notre Dame cathedral, strolled along the Seine and sampled the best vanilla ice cream in the world.

From Paris, we picked up our rental car and headed west to Normandy. As we drove into the region, huge banners hung over the roads for the Fiftieth Anniversary of D-Day celebrations. *Bienvenue Les Américains, Bienvenue Nos Libérateurs.* Welcome Americans, Welcome Our Liberators. The banners featured a photo of two smiling French children, a boy and a girl, held by two American soldiers.

"That could have been Dad and Gilbert," I told Heather as we encountered the banners everywhere. I looked forward to taking part in some of the anniversary celebrations. For my article on French spas, we settled into a seaside spa for a few days of algae wraps, seawater baths, massages and soaks in warm seawater pools. Heather got over some of her post-exams fatigue and we both recovered from some jet lag as we relaxed and unwound.

"This is so cool, Mom," she said.

Our last day in Normandy, Heather and I drove to the American cemetery above Omaha Beach, which was busy with returning soldiers and their families. We overheard a conversation with a guide who was helping an American woman with gray hair find the grave of her husband, who had died in the invasion; we both felt the power and poignancy of that moment.

Heather and I walked along the cliff, which looked down upon Omaha Beach and past the continuous rows of white crosses. Both of us felt the sobering reality that if my father's name had been on one of those crosses, we wouldn't be standing there together.

We then drove to the city of Caen for a ceremony honoring returning soldiers and their families. Heather and I were the only women in the town hall as I lined up, as the daughter of a veteran, with the soldiers or their sons.

The elderly mayor stood in front of each one of us, pinned on a medal and, with tears in his eyes, recited a short speech of gratitude, first in French and then in heavily accented English. I couldn't stop the tears from falling, looking at the old soldiers, remembering Dad and being so touched by the sincere gratitude of the mayor.

After the ceremony, we all stood, shy and awkward, sipping champagne and munching cookies. Heather had not slept well the night before, still getting used to the time difference and was anxious to leave. Between the cemetery and the ceremony, it had also been a moving and emotional day. I thanked the mayor, and Heather and I walked back to our tiny rental car. This was my moment to find the newspaper office and to place the ad to try to find Gilbert Des Clos.

"Just put the seat back and rest, listen to your music and I'll dash down the street and place this ad," I said. I had noticed when we parked that we were on the same street as the news-paper *Ouest France*.

Heather seemed so tired and restless that there was a mo-ment when I thought that maybe I shouldn't take the time. But then I remembered the end of my meeting with the press attaché in San Francisco and her insistence that I might be able to find Gilbert.

"I'll hurry. I have to try," I said. "I promised."

"Okay," she said. She put the seat back and punched in the cassette of her favorite music that she had recorded for the trip. I ran down the street searching for the newspaper's address, then spotted the sign, *Ouest France*. After bounding up the steps two at a time, I burst into the front door, startling the young receptionist seated there.

"Excuse me, I would like to place a *petite annonce* in the newspaper," I said, trying to catch my breath.

"It concerns the war and the anniversary. I'm looking for someone," I added.

Something changed in her face when I said those last words, "*Je cherche quelqu'un*," I'm looking for someone. She paused, then got up from her desk.

"Yes Madame, of course. One moment, if you please." When she returned, she smiled and beckoned for me to follow her.

"Please come this way."

The receptionist ushered me into the office of Monsieur Champion, who stood to welcome me and motioned to a chair. The story tumbled out—of how I was hoping to find the orphan my father tried to adopt fifty years earlier. Monsieur Champion was visibly moved by the tale and reassured me that the newspaper was happy to place the ad at no cost, to appear the following day.

I told him that I was leaving to begin a tour of France with my daughter and because I believed it might take months or even years to find Gilbert, if I found him at all, I gave my home address in California for the ad. I thanked him and excused myself to hurry back to Heather.

I felt relieved that I had fulfilled my promise to the press attaché but sure that my chances of finding my father's orphan were slim at best—I wasn't even sure how to spell his last name.

I lived over five hundred miles from where I grew up, so if someone was looking for me in a Southern California newspaper, they wouldn't find me. But maybe he still was in Normandy, as the press attaché had said.

It was so worth the try and placing the ad was the best chance I had. After all, the press attaché had helped me and she knew. And they had been so kind to me at the newspaper. Heather and I were heading south and east toward more French spas and other delightful adventures in our carefully planned itinerary.

Thinking of the trip ahead and doubting that I would hear from Gilbert Des Clos soon, if at all, I steered our rental car through the winding streets of Caen and left Normandy behind in the rear view mirror.

The next morning, Heather and I awoke in a luxurious room in the Relais De Margaux, near Bordeaux. We spent the day lounging by the pool, reading and then jogging down narrow country lanes lined with vineyards bulging with dark purple grapes. In the evening, we drove two kilometers for dinner at the one quite wonderful restaurant in the nearby village.

19

That same morning, back in Normandy, just a few miles from Caen, Gilbert Des Clos was preparing his early morning cup of strong coffee when the phone rang. His wife Huguette had just left for work and this was his time to sit in his chair, enjoy his coffee and the morning paper.

The jangling of the phone in the hall startled him. Who could be calling this early? Had his wife's car broken down? Or was it his daughter, Cathy? Was one of his grandsons sick?

As he lifted the receiver, he heard his neighbor Pierre shouting: "Gilbert, Gilbert, hurry, you must open the paper. There is a petite annonce. Someone is looking for you."

Gilbert thanked him, hung up the phone, grabbed the paper and searched for the ad. Then he saw it. "The daughter of Lt. Donald K. Johnson looks for Gilbert Des Clos, Du Clos, not sure of the spelling of the last name. During the war, this Naval officer took Gilbert under his wing, and now Johnson's daughter would like to find him. Please write to Diane Covington, P.O. Box 1122, Nevada City, California."

Gilbert slumped down into his chair, put his face into his hands and wept. Could this be possible? After fifty years, could he finally be hearing from his beloved Lieutenant Johnson?

Gilbert had told his wife, his daughter and his grandsons

the stories of those precious months during the war when the kind naval officer took him through the food line every day and even tried to adopt him and take him home to America.

And most of all, Gilbert thought, as the memories flooded back to him, he had learned from Lieutenant Johnson what it meant to be *loved.*

Gilbert had told his family that one day, his American family would come and find him. He wasn't sure if they believed his words, but it seemed like they wanted him to have his story about the loving man who had been the only father he had ever known. After all these years, Gilbert had even wondered at times if *he* had imagined his Lieutenant Johnson, a fantasy father, to help relieve the lonely pain of never being adopted.

For every major anniversary celebration of the D-Day invasion, when American soldiers returned to Normandy, Gilbert waited and hoped. But nothing, year after year. Until now. He dried his tears and read the ad again.

Before he had time to call his wife, four more friends called to make sure he had seen the newspaper. When he finally did reach his wife Huguette, and told her the news, she cried too. She found a copy of the newspaper and called him back, excited to share his joy.

He took a few sips of the now almost cold coffee and calmed himself. His wife told him to call the newspaper office and see if they had any more information about the daughter. Yes, he would do that. He walked to the phone in the hall and, with shaking hands, dialed the number of the office of *Ouest France* and was put through to Monsieur Champion.

Monsieur Champion was thrilled to realize that the American woman's search for her father's French orphan had been fulfilled so quickly. Sadly, he had to tell Gilbert that she had left the area to begin a tour of France. Gilbert felt stunned that he had come so close to reconnecting with his American family and somehow had missed them. He called his wife Huguette back and told her the news.

"Don't worry, we'll write a letter tonight and send it to California. Maybe there's a way that she will find out before she leaves France. Monsieur Champion did say she was planning on staying for a month, remember?"

Gilbert agreed and hung up the phone. But he felt anxious, emotional and unsettled. So many feelings that he had buried for so long now surfaced. He sat down in his chair and leaned back. Images played like movies in his mind, scenes he had relived over and over, so full of comfort and love in the barren landscape of his childhood.

Now he knew that they were real. He had not imagined his Lieutenant Johnson who had loved him. He closed his eyes and let the tears flow.

JUNE 6TH, 1944

Before dawn, Gilbert, age seven, had been awakened by his caretaker, Madame Bisson, and hurried to hide in the root cellar in the garden. Madame Bisson, her granddaughter Georgette, Gilbert's friend and playmate, and Gilbert huddled together, listening to the roar of planes overhead, the blasts of gunfire and feeling the ground shake with the explosion of bombs.

Madame Bisson whispered that this could be the long-awaited invasion they had all prayed for. Friends in the French Underground had said that the English and Americans were going to be landing to fight the Germans. After four years of German occupation, were their prayers finally to be answered?

They stayed in the cellar until late morning. When Madame Bisson peered out, she was startled to see an American paratrooper lying in the dirt among the neatly planted rows of lettuces. She crept out to look and discovered sadly that the young man was unmoving. She hustled the children back into the house and waited for the rest of the day and evening. Gunfire rang out and soldiers ran down the narrow lane beside the house, making it too dangerous to go out.

The next morning, the young man in the garden still had not moved and Madame Bisson knew the worst; he had died fighting for their freedom. A neighbor came by and they all worked together to dig a grave at the back of the garden, draping the soldier in his parachute and laying him gently into the ground. Even Gilbert helped with his own small shovel, feeling the solemnity of the occasion.

Madame Bisson kept the children indoors for almost two weeks, until it seemed as if the fighting had moved farther inland and things had quieted down. Gilbert sat by the window, waiting for the day when he and Georgette would be free again to play and explore outside, hiding in the tall grass and running along the cliffs above the beach below.

He could see from the front window that a camp was springing up just below his house. He ached to get closer and watch. Finally, the day came when Madame Bisson gave him permission to go outside, as long as he didn't go far.

At first light, Gilbert ran to the farthest edge of the yard and sat in the tall grass. He shivered in the brisk sea air as he watched the field below. Such commotion and so many things moving about—Jeeps, trucks, and men carrying huge bags with writing on them. He could smell food cooking nearby from a big tent and breathed in the delicious smells. He put his hand on his thin stomach to stop it from growling.

He ventured down a little closer to where he could see a tall man who held a clipboard and seemed to be in charge. Gilbert noticed how the men in the white caps saluted the other man. Gilbert crept down a little further to watch, then didn't move as the hours passed and the morning turned into mid-day.

Gilbert woke up in his chair and shook his head. He must have dozed off and been dreaming. Then he spotted the open newspaper on the table beside him and remembered. Oh yes, the ad, the daughter, of course. He read it again. It didn't matter that he had already read it dozens of times. He would read it again and again, letting it sink into his brain and his senses. He had waited so long.

Huguette was coming home early from work to help him to write the letter. Then they would take it to the post office and send it to America, to California. Just perhaps it could reach there in time for someone to contact the daughter while she was still in France. They had to try. Every minute seemed to matter.

His daughter Cathy called from work to express her excitement. The whole village knew the story now, it seemed. They were all so happy for Gilbert. Such good news.

Now, if he could just find the daughter.

Many miles south, along the road from Bordeaux to Auch, the next stop on our tour, Heather and I were lost. The French road signs didn't match the map. Added to that, at the roundabout where the road, without warning, became a circle and the destinations spread out like the rays of the sun, the names of those towns also didn't match the map.

Heather wiggled and squirmed in our tiny rental car, groaning as she attempted to stretch her right leg out of the window.

"How much farther till we get there?"

I was trying to read the map and road signs while staying clear of the other cars on the narrow lane. Meanwhile, Heather's music blared from the tape player.

"Heather, could you please turn the music down? I can't think when it is so loud!" She complied but shot me an exasperated look.

We had been driving for hours but seemed to be only half-way to our destination. When I had planned this trip, everyone told me France was the size of Texas. I'd never been to Texas, but it was beginning to dawn on me that it was a lot bigger than I had realized. But what to do? I'd already arranged all of our hotels and we had to drive.

Hours later, we arrived, hot and tired at the Hotel de France, in Auch. We were to dine on succulent duck breast and delectable desserts. The Tour de France bicycle race was passing by, just a few kilometers away, so we got caught up in that excitement.

We had no idea of the drama that was unfolding with Gilbert Des Clos.

That afternoon, Huguette came home early as promised, giving her husband a long hug.

"*Enfin, c'est arrivé.*" Finally, it has happened.

She had always wanted to believe Gilbert's stories of the kind officer who tried to adopt him during the war. At times she even wondered if it was all a fantasy, but what harm would that be, she thought. What lonely child wouldn't want to imagine a person like he had described his lieutenant to be?

But now it was real. And best of all, for Gilbert, a possible reunion with the American family that he almost became a part of, who were trying to find him.

They sat down at the dining table and got out some fine white paper that Huguette reserved for her letters. Together, they composed a three-page emotional letter to the daughter, remembering her father, his love and the time he and Gilbert shared in 1944.

The letter ended with their address, phone, and the hope that this reached her in time for a reunion while she was still in France. They sealed it and walked hand-in-hand to La Poste, a few blocks up in the village, and sent it to America, to California, the fastest way possible.

God speed, thought Huguette as the postmistress took the letter. May it bring back good news to Gilbert. And soon.

Meanwhile, Heather and I found some relief from the long drives by stopping at parks and rest stops to take breaks. With her nineteen-year-old energy and exuberance, she liked to jog around the parks and I kept up as best as I could. In one, we found a giant teeter-totter and laughed and shrieked, hair flying as we sailed through the air, up and down, both feeling about ten years old.

We had looked forward to this trip for years and I so wanted it to turn out well. I kept trying to figure out a solution to the long drives. After visiting Claire in Nice, we faced at least a twelve-hour drive across France to our last destination before Paris, the resort towns of Pornichet and La Baule along the Atlantic coast. And with our penchant for getting lost, it would take us longer. We were both dreading all those hours in the car, so I hatched a plan.

I talked Hertz into allowing us to leave our car in Nice, fly to Nantes, near our destination, and pick up another car there. After all, we would be putting so many fewer miles on the car! It took quite a few phone calls but, to our good fortune, a friendly customer service representative agreed to my plan.

It was a thrill to soar over France, covering in just over an hour the distance that we would have struggled across in the heat in our car. In Nantes, we drove the short drive to our last stop, the towns of Pornichet and La Baule, along the Côte d'Amour, where the wide, sandy beaches reminded us of California.

I had arranged for us to rent a small, furnished apartment where we could settle in for a week. We'd been on the move for two weeks since we left Normandy and it felt good to stop and relax. The area had more of the seawater therapy spas, for my articles.

We'd been in hotels, some large and luxurious and some quaint, with rooms no bigger than the bed, and they'd all been charming. In contrast, now we had our own kitchen, so we could go to the open markets and buy fresh fruits, vegetables and cheese, to the boulangerie for fresh baguettes and pain au chocolat, then go on a picnic or come home to our little place to fix meals, just like the locals.

We were near the end of our trip, so both Heather and I were feeling confident in the language and enjoying the challenges of negotiating day-to-day life in French. It had been so special to have this time together discovering France.

20

My sister Sharon lived a busy life, with a husband and three active children. She fixed healthy meals and drove the kids to all their activities, coming and going in an old red Jeep, with the fake wood paneling on the side. So when I asked her to pick up my mail at my post office box, she agreed to go whenever she could.

On one hectic day, she ran into the post office and gathered the mail. It had been a while, so the box overflowed with letters. One large envelope stood out from the rest, she noticed, as she headed back to the car. She tended to run late and this particular afternoon, was hurrying to get her son home for a violin lesson.

She stashed the mail in the front passenger seat, next to a bag of groceries. Once home, the mail got deposited at the end of the kitchen counter, on top of the red folder labeled "Diane and Heather's Itinerary."

At eight o'clock, after dinner and dishes, she had a moment to stand at the kitchen counter and take a breath. Her eyes caught the large brown envelope in the stack of mail again. Maybe I should look at that, she thought. But then the phone rang and the thought was lost again in the conversation.

It was after nine when, as she straightened up the counter

just before turning off the kitchen light, she saw the corner of the large envelope again in the pile of mail. The stamp looked foreign—was it *French*? She shifted the pile so that she could get a better look.

It *was* a French stamp and the envelope said *par avion*, air-mail. She fished the envelope out of the stack and noticed the neat, feminine handwriting, then read the return address in the upper left hand corner, *Gilbert Des Clos.*

"Oh my God," she said out loud. "Oh my God," she repeated, as she ripped open the envelope, pulled out the letter and started reading the French.

It was *him*. It was the orphan Dad had tried to adopt. Diane had found him. She'd found him. Tears streamed down her cheeks as she read through the letter.

He is real. He is alive. He remembers Dad. Diane said that she was going to try to find him, but I didn't think that she would. I mean, after fifty years?

She remembered how their Dad had talked about Gilbert during her last visit, the summer before he died. The boy had meant a lot to him. She continued to read the letter, feeling the deep emotions behind the words as she made out more of them with her rusty French.

This is amazing. But then she paused. Except that Diane doesn't know about this letter and she's still there. Oh, I hope it is not too late to get this to her somehow. I have to try to let her know. Sharon opened up the folder with the itinerary and checked the calendar on the wall above her, to match up all the dates and places. There was one phone number and fax number for a meeting and luncheon for the next day, the last contact listed.

With the nine-hour time difference, if she could fax the letter, it would get there in time. But who had a fax? A good friend Sarah and her husband had one, so she called them, apologizing for the late hour, told them the story and asked if she could come over and fax the letter back to France.

That would get the fax there in the morning, just in time for Diane to get it when she went to the meeting and luncheon. Sarah and her husband were glad to try to help, so Sharon headed over to their house. It was after eleven before they got the fax to go through, after a few failed tries and figuring out the long-distance country codes. They drank some cognac to celebrate and shared a toast that the letter would find her in time.

But what if she had changed her plans? They all agreed to not think about that, but to imagine the letter somehow getting into Diane's hands, creating a reunion between Diane and Gilbert.

It was all up to fate at this point.

When the tourist office in Pornichet, France, opened at nine the next morning, a stack of faxes waited to be sorted. The young woman whose job it was to get them to the right staff member noticed that a three-page personal letter to a Ms. Covington had been the last fax to come in. From her brief glance, she also saw that the letter seemed very emotional and personal.

Confused by this, she asked her older co-worker what to do. They figured out that the letter was addressed to the American writer who was meeting with their director for a tour and lunch. They'd have to give her the letter if she came back after lunch.

"We need to make sure that she gets this," the young woman said, looking at the letter. "It seems that she has found someone she was looking for—something about her father, a boy and the war."

"All right then, let's make sure someone is here to give it to her if she comes back."

Gilbert and Huguette had been anxious and waiting since the day they mailed the letter to California. They no longer discussed it out loud, but both had the same recurring thoughts. Would Madame Covington find out about the letter in time? If not, when would she come back to France? It could be years.

But they didn't talk about that. They talked about the fact that the month wasn't over yet, that there was still hope. Every time the phone rang, they jumped. But the days and weeks passed and she didn't call.

Heather and I had loved our time in Pornichet and La Baule, a quiet time of swimming at the beach, walking, and exploring the towns and area. We visited two local spas, our favorite French discovery—to be painted again with hot algae and wrapped up to rest, then rinsed off, feeling cleansed and revived.

The trip had turned out better than we could have imagined and we were relaxed and laughing as we packed up and loaded the car. I had one more meeting that morning and our plan was to stop and stay somewhere on the drive back to Paris. Then, after one last night in Paris, we would fly back to California early the following morning.

I noticed that the date was July 20th, my dad's birthday. He would have been eighty that day. I held him in my thoughts as we went about our morning.

Heather came along with me on my tour with the director of the tourist office. We enjoyed lunch at an outdoor café, then walked back to her office to say goodbye. As we turned to leave, a shy young woman came around from the back, a letter in her hand.

"Madame Covington, you have a fax."

I looked at the young woman, puzzled. Who even knew where I was? By then, I'd forgotten all about the itinerary in the red folder on Sharon's kitchen counter. That seemed so long ago, before we had even started our journey.

She handed me the letter. When I glanced at the return address in the top left hand corner, I stopped and said in English, "Oh my God," then started to cry. Everyone waited while I tried to compose myself, but as I kept reading, the tears continued to fall.

"*Qu'est-ce-que c'est?*" What is it? the manager whispered.

I told her briefly how I'd placed the ad to try to find my father's French orphan and that this was a letter from him, the first communication in fifty years. She took a quick breath in and took charge.

"Madame Covington, you must come right now and call him. Do not wait another minute," she said, taking my arm and leading me into the back office. Everyone stood and watched as the story spread in whispered tones.

I sat down at her desk and picked up the phone with a shaking hand. What would I say? How would I begin? It doesn't matter, I thought. Just call. I dialed the number and heard it ringing. Then a man answered.

"*Allo?*" I took a breath and began.

"*Gilbert? C'est Diane, ici, Diane Covington, la fille de Donald.*" Gilbert? It's Diane here. Diane Covington, the daughter of Donald.

I fought back the emotions that tightened my throat and heard him take a sharp breath in—he was crying too. We both stammered through the conversation. We sorted out that yes, I was still in France. He wanted to know if we could meet. I turned to Heather. She nodded.

Gilbert invited us to come back to Normandy to meet them and to spend the night. I agreed and took down the name of a café in Caen where we could rendezvous later that afternoon.

I set down the phone and stared, still stunned. What if I hadn't come back to the office after lunch? What if we'd changed our plans? How had Sharon managed to fax me this letter? But she *had* managed to fax the letter and we *hadn't* changed our plans.

I sighed and smiled at all the office staff who waited, talking quietly, some of them wiping away tears. As I said goodbye to them and thanked the tourist office director, she gripped my hand hard.

"*Bonne chance avec la réunion.*" Good luck with the reunion.

"*Merci.*"

Outside in the bright midday sun, I tried to remember where I'd parked the car. The world had shifted since earlier that morning. I'd found Gilbert. I still couldn't believe it. We were on our way to meet him. *Oh Dad, if only you could have been here for this.*

Heather and I found our car and headed for the main road for the three-hour drive back to Normandy. I appreciated Heather's willingness for the detour, knowing it added extra hours of driving.

"Of course, Mom. You have to go," she said, when I thanked her.

As we drove along, I worried a bit. What if they were not nice people? That would be one thing if I was alone, but I was taking Heather there. Yet the letter was so beautifully written, and sweet. The way he described his memories of Dad was so touching. They must be good people. And talking to him on the phone, it felt right to go. I just had to trust.

We followed the signs back to Caen and Heather helped me with the map. We'd come so far since the beginning of the trip, now working together as a team. She'd taught me all the words to her favorite songs on her tape and I'd taught her some old Frank Sinatra standards from my childhood—"All The Way" and "When I Fall in Love." We sang together, windows down, our voices carried on the breezes, out over the fields of sunflowers and grain.

We arrived in Caen a few minutes early and found the café where we were to meet Gilbert. As we sat and waited, I fidgeted in my metal café chair, searching the faces of people passing by. Could it really be possible that I was waiting to meet Gilbert Des Clos, the boy from my childhood stories? And how would I know him?

All around us, the French took long puffs on their Galois cigarettes. They were all having an ordinary day, a coffee at four o'clock, or a glass of wine, before heading home to their normal life. But my life did not feel normal at all; it felt surreal, like I'd shifted back in time to the yellow Formica table with my father and his stories of France.

Except that now I was in the story too, about to meet his special orphan. And it wasn't the past, but the present. I was no longer a child and neither was Gilbert. My mind whirled.

I had never smoked, but right then, wished I could grab a cigarette and light up, just to have something to do with my hands. We waited. Then a trim, well-dressed man walked up to us, smiled and said my name, "*Diane*," which he pronounced "*Deeahhne*," and held out his hand.

"*Gilbert*," he said simply, then gave me four kisses, the warm greeting of Normandy, reserved for special family and friends. His wife Huguette, stood right behind him, smiling, then greeted both Heather and me the same way.

Gilbert, Huguette and I stood, awkward and crying, trying to compose ourselves in the crowded café. Huguette handed out tissues. I don't remember the first words we said to each other. I do remember that when I looked into Gilbert's eyes, I saw the same soft expression of kindness that Dad always had; Gilbert, though not as tall as Dad, actually resembled him somehow.

But he wasn't related to Dad. What was I thinking? Yet from that first moment, Gilbert felt like family. He told me that he knew who I was because I looked so much like my dad. After fifty years, he remembered what my dad had looked like, enough to recognize me.

We decided to go back to their home, where we could talk more easily, and discussed where to meet on the street so that Heather and I could follow behind their car. I kept realizing I was talking to Gilbert so normally, discussing directions.

This was real. Gilbert was real. I had found him.

21

Gilbert and Huguette lived in Colombelles, a small village a short drive from Caen. Their home, a sturdy stone building over two hundred years old, had been in Huguette's family for generations; Huguette had been born there.

Just inside the entrance hall, across from where coats, boots and umbrellas were organized, the telephone sat on a small table. Behind the hall, a tiny kitchen connected to the garden by way of a laundry room, where Huguette kept finches in a cage just inside the door to the garden. Their dog, Elliott, a stray that they had adopted, barked an excited greeting as we entered the house.

To the right, in the joint living room and dining room, the dining table took up most of the space. On the couch, against the wall under the stairs and facing the television, their cat, Couscous, slept curled up on a crocheted blanket. She too was rescued from the animal shelter.

Once inside, our first surprise was that the little boy held by the American soldier in the photo on the banner that we had seen everywhere *was* Gilbert. And his friend, Georgette, Madame Bisson's granddaughter, was the little girl in the poster. An American soldier had sent the snapshot back for the fiftieth anniversary and Gilbert had recognized himself. It was the only photo he had from his childhood.

A large framed copy of the poster sat on a shelf behind the table. Gilbert described how he saw the banners and couldn't believe it was he and Georgette. The photo also led to a re-union with Georgette, who had been lost to him since the war. Georgette, like Gilbert, still lived in Normandy. On the wall behind the couch, another framed photo of their grandsons, Romain and Benoit, had the place of honor.

Gilbert carried our suitcases up the narrow wooden stairs and placed them in the guest room where Heather and I were to sleep. The simple, clean room, with ironed, embroidered sheets and pillowcases, had a crucifix over the bed, a television and a metal clothes rack.

When we came back down, Gilbert opened a bottle of chilled champagne and we sat out in the garden to sip it and to chat. The conversation felt light and friendly. We had the whole evening ahead and the next day to talk. I mentioned that it was Dad's birthday and we toasted him together. How perfect that I had found Gilbert on Dad's special day. Dad had celebrated his thirtieth birthday in France, with Gilbert. Now Gilbert and I were remembering Dad together on what would have been his eightieth.

Gilbert was retired from his job and spent his days tending a huge plot in a community vegetable garden nearby. Each day he brought home a basket of freshly harvested produce and Huguette made a fresh potage, or vegetable soup, for the first course of their dinner.

Huguette worked in a nearby hospital in the accounting office and had left work early that day to meet us in Caen. Somehow she had prepared a delicious dinner, the potage and a green salad from Gilbert's garden, Coquille Sainte-Jacques, with seafood fresh from the nearby Atlantic, bread and wine, with a cheese board for dessert. After dinner, she brought out a box of chocolates and a dusty bottle of Calvados, the local hard cider, which I remembered Dad describing as "firewater."

Cathy, Gilbert's daughter, and her two small sons, Benoit, five and Romain, nine, joined us in the evening for dinner. I told them all about the article I'd written for the 50th anniversary, how I'd sent it to the French Consulate, and how the press attaché had encouraged me to place the ad. We all marveled again at our good fortune to be together.

As we sat and chatted, crowded into their cozy living and dining room, I was grateful that my reunion with Gilbert came at the end of the trip. I'd had three-and-a-half weeks to let French seep into my brain and my heart, to listen, to learn, to speak and be understood. Even so, Huguette reminded Cathy to speak *plus doucement*, more slowly, to be sure that we could follow. Cathy had an excited energy and tended to talk fast.

As we talked, I realized that all the years of French classes and videos and countless hours studying vocabulary and irregular verbs had been for this moment, so that I could find and communicate with Gilbert Des Clos and his family.

I saw then that my ongoing passion for French and France had a deeper purpose than I could have ever imagined. Thank God I had held onto my dream. I knew that Dad would have been so proud—and amazed.

Gilbert asked questions about Dad, about our lives and about how Dad had died. When I told him that I had grown up hearing the stories about him and that Dad had talked about him again just before he died, Gilbert looked away and tried to compose himself, but couldn't stop the tears. I could tell that for Gilbert, who had never been adopted, knowing that Dad had never forgotten him meant everything.

Gilbert told me about his lonely years in the orphanage, waiting and hoping that somehow, Dad would come back for him. Then, in his teens, a kind woman took him in to live with her family and her love and nurturing helped him to gain confidence and strength.

He went into the military, served time in Vietnam, then came home and worked in a factory job for many years. When he met and married his wife Huguette in his early twenties, and they had their daughter Cathy, life took on meaning and depth.

"My life began again with my family," he said. "It was the most important thing." I flashed back to my time in Hawaii with Dad, when I was eighteen, when he had said the very same words. I shivered, feeling the power of this meeting with this man, such a link to my father.

He told me the same stories Dad had told, but from a child's perspective. He talked of his excitement upon visiting the Navy camp and his fascination with the huge ships, where they sometimes ate lunch if Dad was busy down at the beach. He told how he loved zipping around in the Jeep and that Dad had even taught him the basics of how to drive it.

He talked about how Dad carried a gun, a fact that Dad had never mentioned. Listening to his stories gave me back some more pieces of my father and I was grateful.

He described the wonder of the delicious food that fed his body, day after day. But the most important memory he had was how Dad's love had nurtured his spirit. Remembering Dad's strong arms around him, he wept again. We sat together, silent and moved, missing the father who had loved us both.

After dinner, Gilbert uncorked the dusty bottle of Calvados. As we sipped the powerful cider, he became more serious, and seemed to be getting up his courage to talk to me about something else. Didn't I know the whole story already? I'd heard it so many times from Dad and now from Gilbert.

But nothing could have prepared me for what Gilbert was about to tell me.

Gilbert took a gulp of his Calvados, leaned forward and told me his version of that late October day in 1944, when he and Dad had to say goodbye.

Dad knelt down and held him close. Gilbert hung on tight, sobbing and burying his head in Dad's thick, wool Navy coat. Cold October winds whipped around them as men rushed by, carrying their heavy sea bags on their shoulders, excited to be going home.

It was time to say goodbye. As Dad stood up, Gilbert clung tight to his legs. Dad looked out at the waiting ship, then turned and spoke to Gilbert.

"Do you want to go home with me to America?" Dad asked.

Gilbert murmured "*Oui*."

Dad picked him up and hoisted him onto his hip, as he'd done so many times and held him tight as they hopped into a Jeep for the trip down to the beach. As they boarded the ship, the captain, who'd been watching, shook his head.

"Johnson, off the record, if you're caught, I know nothing about this."

Dad nodded, shifting Gilbert's weight.

Within the hour, storm winds raged. Twenty-foot waves lashed the hull of the huge ship. They would not be able to cross the English Channel until the seas calmed. The storm lasted throughout the day and night.

The next morning, as the sun rose, the wind slackened and sailors scurried about, readying the ship for departure. Moments before the ship was to cast off, French gendarmes pulled up on the beach, demanding to speak with the captain. Madame Bisson had reported that her ward had not returned home and they were looking for him.

The captain called for my father. After a long, strained pause, the lieutenant appeared at the top of the gangplank, carrying the sleepy boy in his arms. Gilbert rubbed his eyes in the bright sunlight. When he saw the gendarmes, he hid his head and clung to Dad.

"*Non!*" he wailed, "*Non.*" Dad walked down the gangplank, then knelt down on the sand with Gilbert. The gendarmes had to pull the boy away.

Madame Bisson placed him in an orphanage that night.

Gilbert replaced the cork in the Calvados bottle.

"Your father said he would come back for me. I have been waiting for fifty years for some word from him."

I sat, stunned. First that Dad had taken Gilbert onto the ship. He had never told us that part of the story. Then that Dad had promised to come back. He had never mentioned that either.

The cat was awake now and enjoying being petted by Romain, who listened intently to the conversation, his eyes wide and his head turning back and forth between us. Benoit had fallen asleep on the couch, next to the dog. I took another sip of my Calvados, trying to absorb these new facts.

We sat together in an awkward silence until Cathy asked, "Why didn't he? Why didn't he come back?"

Her tone was not exactly hostile, but it also wasn't warm. I could see what she meant. If my father had risked taking Gilbert onto the ship and then promised to come back for him, how could he not have kept that promise? How could you let a child down like that? I couldn't think of what to say in English, let alone French.

Then after a moment, Cathy whispered, "*Le destin.*" Destiny. It was Gilbert's destiny to stay in France and have his life there, so that he could marry Huguette, and Cathy could be born, and her sons.

We sat together in the small living room, feeling the mystery of life and how we can't always understand, until we look back, why things happen the way that they do. After Cathy and her sons left and Heather went up to bed, Huguette, Gilbert and I sat together, talking until late. When we said good-night, Gilbert took my hands, his eyes bright with tears.

"I always knew that someday I would hear from your father, that someone would come," he said. "Thank you."

We stood for a moment, both moved and grateful for the destiny that had brought us together. I climbed the narrow wooden stairs to the guest bedroom where Heather lay sleeping and slipped into bed. The shutters on the old window rattled with a wind off the sea, as I lay awake, going over all that had happened that afternoon.

I'd found Gilbert Des Clos. We were sleeping in his house. He remembered Dad, even told the same stories. All of that felt amazing and gave me another link to Dad, with this emotional connection from his past and the war.

But the rest of the story, that Dad had never talked about. How desperate he must have been to take Gilbert onto the ship, to take such a risk. And how—why—had he carried that secret for his whole life?

Why hadn't he told us? Had he wanted to hide that he'd been willing to defy the rules? And what about his promise to come back for Gilbert? He'd never mentioned that either. Was he ashamed that he didn't fulfill his promise? Was my mother against the idea and was it just another subject that they argued about at night, when they thought we couldn't hear?

I could see my father and Gilbert on that windy, desolate beach and imagine the tug of the gendarmes pulling a part of Dad's heart away as they took the boy. I punched my pillow into a new shape and stared at the rough wood beams in the ceiling.

Why hadn't I paid more attention to how important this had been to Dad? But then, Dad had kept the real heart of the story hidden, what Gilbert had just told me. If I'd known that, would I have realized the depth of their connection? And why hadn't I helped Dad to find Gilbert earlier, while there was still time for him to be here with us now?

As the clock ticked on the bedside table and the hours passed, I realized I could find no answers from the past. But I'd found Gilbert again. We could go forward from here.

There was an aura of Dad about Gilbert. I noticed it in the way he patiently explained a game to his grandson, in his pride in his garden's bounty and in the concern he showed that Heather and I knew our way back to Paris.

When we left the next afternoon, Gilbert insisted on driving ahead of us to the freeway onramp to make sure we took the right one. Then he pulled over and stood beside his car, waving till we were out of sight, oblivious to the cars whizzing by, his slight figure silhouetted against the sky.

Could he have known that's exactly what Dad would have done? How had he become so like him, when they'd been together only four months? It was as if their bond had been so deep that Gilbert had soaked up Dad and decided, "I will be like this man."

I wiped away more tears as I waved out the window and watched Gilbert getting smaller and smaller in the rear view mirror. When we said goodbye that day, I vowed that we would never lose touch again.

Dad had been unable to keep his promise. I would make sure that I kept mine.

22

Back in California, Heather and I shared all our adventures with my sister Sharon, who was thrilled that she had been able to play such an important role in our reunion with Gilbert.

I told her about Gilbert's stories from his child's perspective and how Dad had taken him onto the ship, intending to bring him back. And that Dad had promised to come back for Gilbert. She looked as surprised as I'd been about that new part of the story.

"Did Dad ever tell you that?" I asked.

"Never, not a word. Only that he tried to adopt Gilbert and cared about him."

"Why would Dad have kept that part of the story secret?" I asked.

"Maybe he was shocked at his own actions, at his own desperation and at the risk that he had taken," she said.

"I guess we'll never know." I shook my head.

While Heather and I were on our trip, my sister had a seizure. In order to rule out a brain tumor, she had an M.R.I., but to everyone's horror, they did find a tumor. She broke the news to us as soon as we came home. How could my healthy and strong sister, whom I jogged with in the morning, chatting and laughing as we made our way down the road, how could she possibly have a brain tumor?

So mixed with the joy and wonder of our trip and of finding Gilbert, we all felt the shock and fear of this new development. But in a way, talking about the trip gave her a diversion from her serious health challenge. We talked often about the reunion and relished all the details together.

The next time I saw my mother, I related Gilbert's story of being on the ship, ready to come back with Dad to America. Had Dad told her about that? She was sitting up in bed, doing a crossword puzzle, her favorite pastime.

"Yes, that is true," she said, not looking up. "The captain told him that if he got caught, that he was on his own." I couldn't believe that she had also known that part of the story and yet neither she nor Dad had ever mentioned it.

"But wouldn't he have gotten into trouble, just bringing Gilbert onto the ship like that?" I asked her.

"I'm sure he would have," she answered, turning to look up a word in her paperback dictionary. "But he must not have been thinking about that then."

I could tell by the sharp tone of her voice that she didn't want to discuss it any further. If I pushed, I could get clobbered with her anger again.

"No, I guess not," I said.

How mysterious life is, I thought. A storm had changed the destinies of both Gilbert and my father, and then my life, too, because I had been compelled to try and find him.

My mother's life as a single woman, especially as she got older, hadn't turned out quite as she may have planned. My father had happily remarried, but my mother had not had a successful long-term relationship since their divorce. After I found Gilbert, I noticed that she put my father's navy photo from 1944 on her bedside table again.

She also started referring to herself as a widow, another example of bending reality to fit her own needs. But she seemed interested, not only that I'd found Gilbert, but in going to France on the next trip to meet him. Mom was excited that the upcoming trip involved a big party, with her in the place of honor.

Gilbert and Huguette were very excited to meet my mother and must have imagined her to be kind and loving. After all, the woman married to my father must be just like him, right? Luckily, the language barrier and the distance helped keep that fantasy alive and I wrote all my mother's messages for her in French.

I kept my word to stay in touch with Gilbert and Huguette. We exchanged letters often, their responses in Huguette's neat, feminine handwriting. I could imagine them sitting at their dining room table and composing the letters together. We chatted on the phone from time to time to talk and for birthdays—Gilbert's and mine were one day apart.

That first Christmas, everyone at Huguette's work chipped in to buy them a fax machine so that we could exchange letters faster, without the week to ten days that mail took to travel between California and France. I bought a fax machine too.

We exchanged simple Christmas gifts. Huguette sent me a cross-stitched tree ornament, which we placed on our tree. It felt right to include them in our thoughts during our family celebrations.

The next spring, 1995, my article about traveling for the month with Heather, "Two for the Road," came out in a major newspaper travel section in California, on Mother's Day. On the 50th anniversary of V.E. day, or Victory in Europe Day that same month, my story "Finding Gilbert" also came out in several newspapers, describing the emotional reunion with my French "brother."

I sent a copy to the press attaché at the French Consulate in San Francisco, thanking her for her part in helping me to find Gilbert. I also sent a copy to Gilbert and Huguette, knowing an English-speaking friend could translate it for them. In my correspondence with Gilbert and his wife, we were planning a special reunion and fête in France, June 1996. My mother and my sister Sharon were planning to go, and Heather wanted to come again too.

After the reunion in Normandy with Gilbert, I planned an itinerary where we visited the spa near their home for five days of the seawater treatments we had so loved. Then a rail/drive trip, which included Mont Saint-Michel, touring the châteaux country and spending three nights in a castle. Then back up to Paris on the train, with some time for shopping and sightseeing. A close friend and her daughter were joining us for the tour after the reunion.

Sharon had been trying various natural and non-traditional therapies for her brain tumor: magnetic therapy, shark cartilage and Reiki, among other things. The doctors recommended surgery and radiation, but Sharon refused. When we first planned for her to go on the trip, she seemed all right.

But as the months passed, she became very forgetful and spacey, which was worrisome. She was to fly over to France with my mother, which was good. Maybe the trip and the spa treatments would help her. I hoped so.

The night before our departure, I received an envelope from the travel agent with Eurail passes for Heather and me. I was sitting on my bed, going over the last minute packing details when I heard my father's voice clearly in my head, saying one of his favorite sayings: *Check and double check.* My eyes fell on the envelope from the travel agent again.

All right Dad, I will check, I half-groaned, laughing at the same time that I seemed to be listening to him "from the other side." But when I opened the envelope, I gasped. Somehow, I had the rail passes for my friend and her daughter—she had Heather's and mine. Thank goodness I had checked.

Heather and I were leaving ahead of the others and couldn't have used rail passes that didn't match our passports. My friend and her daughter's rail passes would have also been invalid. That would have meant a huge loss of money, not to mention the confusion of having to buy train tickets; my friend didn't speak French. Instead, a quick phone call and it all got sorted out in minutes.

Thank you Dad, I mumbled, truly grateful and in awe that I'd heard him like that. Did he know that we were going back to see Gilbert? Such mystery.

Gilbert and his family created a moving and memorable fête in our honor. Fifty of their friends and relations came out for a whole day of feasting and celebrating in the decorated town hall of their village. The mayor showed up to shake hands and share a glass of champagne. The newspaper, *Ouest France*, sent a reporter who scribbled down names and facts and took photos.

I translated for my mother, Heather and Sharon practiced their French and we laughed and smiled all day. It was a wonder to see how much Gilbert's friends and extended family shared his delight at finally finding his American family and how much the story meant to them, too.

For Gilbert, it was the fulfillment of a dream to meet my mother and Sharon, two more members of his American family and to share the wonder of our reunion with his family and friends. My mother was honored as Dad's wife; although Gilbert and Huguette knew about my parents' divorce, no one mentioned it.

We gathered in the late morning for champagne. Then about noon we sat down to eat. Sharon, Mom and I sat at a head table with Gilbert and Huguette. Huguette, with help from a few friends, orchestrated the serving of course after course from the kitchen in the hall.

The village of Colombelles is located just a few kilometers from the Atlantic, so we enjoyed many courses of *fruits de mer*, fresh seafood, which I learned the words for—mussels, *les moules*, lobster, *homard*, clams and oysters, *les huîtres*, and crab, *le crabe*. Those creatures were swimming in the English Channel just hours before they ended up on our plates.

Huguette had been cooking for weeks and storing food at her neighbors' homes. Quiches, hors d'oeuvres, salads, tarts. Friends brought dishes that they'd created, including varied and luscious desserts—cakes, crêpes and ice cream.

We brought presents for the family and Gilbert's grandsons, Romain, now eleven and Benoit, seven, loved their "Wilson" t-shirts so much that they promptly put them on over their formal clothes. I filled my head with the language while my belly filled with champagne and food and my heart with all the love that was pouring out to us.

People moved about and chatted with each other between courses. Gilbert made several speeches and toasts, with glasses raised and much cheering. Children ran around on the grass outside. At three o'clock in the afternoon, we all stood to take a breather before the dessert course.

Heather, at twenty-one, sat with the young people, talking and laughing. After our trip two years before, when we found Gilbert, she spent six weeks the following summer in Annecy, staying with a family. This was now her third trip to France in three years and she spoke French well.

My mother smiled and enjoyed the food and drink, but the language barrier limited her participation. I translated for her, editing or embellishing her responses, to make her appear, when necessary, more gracious and grateful for their thoughtfulness.

By three, she had clearly had too much to drink and we shuttled her home and upstairs to bed. Everyone was kind, blaming it on her age, eighty, or the jet lag.

By five o'clock, many of the guests had left, but a smaller core group remained. My sister and Heather had joined my mother back at the house, so I was the only member of the family still at the fête. Though hard to imagine, there was to be another light meal that evening.

It really is a wonder how the French stay so slim. But I wanted to stay to the very end to honor all their efforts. Gilbert, Huguette and I headed back to their home about nine that night.

When the newspaper article came out in *Ouest France* later that week, the headline read, "*Sa famille Américaine est enfin arrivée.*" His American family has finally arrived. Gilbert beamed at the article, which included a photo of us all lined up on the grass outside the town hall.

Mom, Sharon, Heather and I stayed with Gilbert and Huguette for an extra week, with Gilbert acting as our chauffeur, driving us each morning to the spa and picking us up each afternoon. Huguette coddled and cared for us, preparing breakfast and dinner each day. Many days, she packed us a lunch to take with us for our noon meal. We sat on the beach and savored cheese, bread, cold cuts and fruit, and sipped wine.

At the spa, my mother received a lot of attention for her age, which she loved. My sister adored the treatments and pampering and Heather and I were thrilled to be back again where we'd been two years before. Gilbert and Huguette joined us at the spa on the last day to soak in the warm seawater pools.

During our stay, Gilbert took us to the house he had lived

in with Madame Bisson and Georgette, just above the camp. That day, we also visited the American Cemetery again—such a powerful and moving experience.

Gilbert and Huguette had purchased an English/French dictionary, which sat on top of the television, right next to the dining table. When we reached a word that I didn't know, I'd look it up and show it to them and then we'd all smile, another piece of understanding reached between us. Most of the time we did well, but having the dictionary helped. They still spoke only a few words of English, "hello," "goodbye" and "thank you."

On our last day, Gilbert and Huguette drove us to the train station to begin the rail and drive trip that I'd so carefully planned. The one glitch, however, was that the trains didn't run to Mont Saint-Michel that day.

We sat at the train station, with no train to board, trying to figure out what to do. Then Gilbert and Huguette volunteered to drive us the one-and-a-half-hour drive, even though it meant they each drove one of their cars, to take us all.

At Mont Saint-Michel, we spent the day together climbing the narrow cobblestone streets to the church at the top, marveling at the dramatic views from the steep stone ramparts down to the sea below. Sharon was having trouble that day, wobbling some when she walked, so Huguette stayed with her while the rest of us hiked to the top.

Late in the afternoon, we all shared a coffee in a café and then it was time to say goodbye. After tearful kisses all around, Gilbert and Huguette headed back home. The next morning, the six of us boarded the train to begin our trip through the château country and then back to Paris.

The rest of the trip went well. We all took turns helping out with Sharon, who had good days, which we enjoyed, and bad days, which were alarming. We were all paying our own way and even though I'd spent weeks arranging all the details of the trip, my mother never once offered to buy me a coffee, let alone lunch or dinner. The sadder fact is that I never expected it. But I was in charge, translating for her, so she was on good behavior and there were no raging arguments.

She especially enjoyed traveling with Heather and at one point I realized that Heather and my mother had never had a chance to bond. Then I realized that it was no wonder: I'd never bonded with my mother either. Yet taking my mother to meet Gilbert seemed to create a new opening in our relationship and I was grateful for that.

I called Gilbert and Huguette from Paris for one last goodbye and thank you for such a warm and welcoming visit. We were already planning their visit to California the following spring.

Gilbert was finally making his trip to America.

Part V

1997

23

Sharon's decreasing physical abilities on the trip had been an indication of what we'd all been afraid of—her brain tumor had grown at an alarming rate. Sharon underwent emergency brain surgery right after returning from France. She elected to not do radiation after the surgery, even though the surgeon warned that the tumor would most likely grow back.

After the surgery and her recovery, Sharon seemed like herself again, which was such a relief and a source of joy. Maybe she was going to be all right. We all felt hopeful and grateful to have bought more time. I kept Gilbert and Huguette up on all the developments and they sent their love and support to Sharon and to all of us.

We stayed in contact by fax and phone, as we planned their two-week visit for the following spring, April 1997. They were coming with their daughter Cathy and Romain and Benoit. Our whole family buzzed with excitement as we arranged the many dinners, picnics and gatherings to celebrate them.

We were gathering both in Northern and Southern California, with the bigger events in the south, where most of the family lived. My mother, in an unprecedented show of generosity, arranged to pay for their stay near her home and for a formal dinner and a few other events. She seemed excited to play her role as hostess and Mamie Bonnye, Grandmother Bonnye.

In April, I met the Des Clos family at the airport in San Francisco and began a fun-filled tour of the city. We took the glass elevator at the Hyatt in Union Square, gasping as we whizzed up on the outside of the building and marveling at the views of the city and San Francisco Bay. We hopped onto the cable cars, toured Fisherman's Wharf, and walked through Chinatown, spending two days in the city to be sure to have time to take in all the sights.

They felt right at home at the Boudin bakery where we found "real" French baguettes, then savored their first American hamburgers at a fifties diner, where Romain and Benoit wiggled with excitement at the free cardboard "classic car" gifts that came with their meal.

They gasped as we drove down Lombard Street, known as the "crookedest street in the world," then over the Golden Gate Bridge to Sausalito and Marin County, where we lunched with a dear friend in her eighties who had lived in Paris in the 1930's. Then home to Nevada City, in the foothills of the Sierras, where we relaxed for a week's stay.

In Nevada City, a California Gold Rush town that dates back to the 1850's, they stayed at a bed and breakfast, right on the quaint main street, exploring the historical town and all the shops, when we weren't off on excursions.

We took picnics to the Yuba River, appreciating the colorful spring wild flowers, and toured the Empire goldmine in the area. My sister and her family drove them to Lake Tahoe for the day and on another night, we shared a family dinner at a restaurant in town, thirteen of us in all.

My nephew Brendan and Gilbert's grandson Romain were both twelve, and Romain wanted to visit Brendan's school. After sitting in the classroom and touring the school, Romain joined in a soccer game at recess. By the end of the visit, Romain declared that he wanted to come to live in California—he thought that the schools were much less formal than in France and the kids had way more fun.

Just before Gilbert and Huguette arrived, my sweet elderly neighbors who owned the apple farm up the hill passed away. By a miraculous series of events, I was able to buy the farm and was in escrow. We walked the property together and looked it over and Gilbert offered to come back and help me with the work needed to restore it. I so appreciated his offer.

Our last evening in Nevada City, we gathered at a friend's home for a farewell party. About thirty friends came with food, several played guitars and we sang, ate and celebrated. Some folks dusted off their college French and other times, I translated for our French family, who appreciated the warmth of it all.

For the hour-long trip to the Sacramento airport the next morning, my friend Sarah rented us a limousine. We all piled in, marveling at the luxurious fun of sipping champagne as we whizzed along. Romain and Benoit especially enjoyed the fun as the eleven of us traveled together to join the rest of the family in the south.

As I sat next to Gilbert for the short flight to San Diego, he tapped his sugar packet on one side, then turned it over and tapped it again on the other side, before adding it to his coffee. I had never seen anyone do that except my dad.

In La Jolla, where my mother lived, the rest of the extended family, forty members in all and spanning four generations, gathered for the weekend to welcome and honor our French family. At one picnic, we all played soccer—Gilbert and my brothers, my nephews and his grandsons, Heather and I—the international game needing no translation.

At a formal dinner hosted by my mother, Gilbert stood up

and, with shaking hands, read a letter he'd composed. I stood next to him and held his other hand, translating his words for him. He thanked everyone, remembering Dad and expressing his wonder at finally fulfilling his dream to come to America and meet his family. Even my mother cried during the touching speech.

As we all talked and visited after dinner, Gilbert's grandsons and my three nephews, similar in age, tired of all the formality, jumped into the community pool at my mother's condominium complex, right outside where we were gathered.

The boys whooped and hollered as they romped and splashed in their underwear, their clothes piled up alongside the pool. We all giggled, enjoying their exuberance, even though we had to shush them a bit—it was after hours for the pool.

While in the San Diego area, we visited Sea World and kissed dolphins, and drove across the bay to Coronado Island. We rode the trolley down to Tijuana, Mexico for the day, where Cathy demonstrated a distinct talent at bargaining for turquoise jewelry. They sampled their first Mexican food, the spicy tacos and enchiladas a bit curious to them, but relished the novelty of being able to journey to Mexico and back in one day.

After San Diego, we headed north to Los Angeles. I thought they might enjoy Disneyland, but they were more interested in seeing Beverly Hills, so we drove down Rodeo drive and through the neighborhoods of expensive homes, then past the Hollywood sign, which they had seen in so many movies.

They wanted to go to Universal Studios, so we spent another day squealing on the rides and marveling at the behind-the-scenes technology of movie making.

At my brother Kenton's house one afternoon, his sons and Gilbert's grandsons, the pool-caper culprits reunited, ran past the adults, giggling and excited. As we chatted and sipped tea and coffee, they played basketball, then swam in the pool and played Nintendo.

Finally, Romain and Benoit dressed up in my nephews' baseball uniforms, proudly showing us all, and tried their hands at baseball. Once again, it didn't seem to matter that the boys didn't speak each other's language. They were speaking the universal language of being boys, of fun and youthful enthusiasm.

As Gilbert and his family took it all in, I witnessed America and California through their eyes—our huge freeways, our giant American cars and trucks, our contrasts of wide-open spaces and dense cities, our fast-paced life—and saw it all newly.

Their return flight left from Los Angeles, so after our busy and joyous two weeks we said goodbye, promising to see each other soon, our connection deeper and more solid.

We were a true family now. Their three French generations had joined with our four American generations in a strong bond of love and understanding that bridged language and cultural differences.

24

The following spring, 1998, I returned to France in early June, to visit Gilbert and Huguette and to write more articles. I hadn't packed a raincoat and got caught in a storm walking to the train station, so when I arrived at their home, damp and bedraggled, I had a bad cold. Huguette took one look at me, clucked like a mother hen and announced, *"Je m'occupe de toi."* I'm going to take care of you.

She bundled me into the car and drove to the shopping center near their home to buy me a raincoat. After cruising through a few stores, we found a nice blue and green coat and I tried it on. She made me turn around, pulling on it, making sure it fit just right, then insisted on paying for it.

Back home, she coddled me with warm drinks and scolded me into naps. It felt delicious and sweet. I'd never been mothered like that and I left feeling closer to them than ever.

Two years had passed since my sister Sharon's brain surgery. After a year where she seemed to be doing better, her symptoms returned and she started acting confused again. The surgeon's prediction had come true—Sharon's brain tumors had grown back. Just after my return from France, she underwent another surgery and this time, elected to do the radiation. We all hoped and prayed again that she would be cured.

In the midst of her radiation treatment, her husband decided to leave. She couldn't function completely on her own, so I became more and more involved, helping her to move into an apartment and to begin her new life.

Sharon faced all of her challenges with grace, which made me cherish her even more. I was so grateful that I lived nearby and could provide some support for her. Her love and warmth, even in the midst of her own huge life changes, were such a gift in my life.

As I celebrated my fiftieth birthday that fall, hitting the half-century point woke me up to my unfulfilled and long-buried dream of living in France. As 1998 turned over into 1999, the last year before the new millennium, I felt the strong stirrings of that dream surface again. My French was strong, thanks to all the visits with Gilbert and Huguette.

Could it still be possible? Was there a way? And if not now, when?

In 1999, as I considered the possibility of living in France, I was invited on two trips to France, in January and again in May, to research and write travel articles. Counting my trip in 1998, I'd been there three times in twelve months and the longing to live there increased.

At that point, Sharon was stable, living in town with two of her children helping her out. It felt like a window opened up in which I might be able to get away for eight months. Before Sharon's condition got worse, I needed to go while I could.

I set the intention that by fall, I would begin my "junior year abroad, thirty years late" and celebrate the new millennium living in France for as many months as I could arrange.

On the spring trip, I spent two days in Aix-en-Provence, near Marseilles, walking the winding cobblestone streets that led to the central square, with its 13th century clock tower that tolled the hour. Over fifty fountains flowed throughout the city.

This was where I would live when I came to stay, I decided. Though I knew no one there, it *felt right* and I trusted that. I returned home to set my plan in motion.

The months, weeks and days sped by and my proposed date to leave, November 3rd, loomed ahead. For my eight-month stay in France, I found a renter for my house, bought a laptop, and put my bills online.

I had some coaching clients that I could work with long distance and some articles lined up to write—enough work to just squeak by. I also had a home equity loan as a safety net; my little apple farm was helping to send me to France.

I said goodbye to family and friends and headed to San Francisco for the flight to Paris. The hardest part was saying goodbye to my new little granddaughter, Ellie. But my son-in-law Claude encouraged me to not put off the trip any longer.

"You have your whole life to be a grandma," he said. "You should go."

He was right. He and my daughter Michelle promised to come over for a visit in the spring. I took one compact rolling bag, and a small backpack. Why take clothes to France, the fashion capital of the world?

As the big jet lumbered down the runway, then rose into the sky, I could see San Francisco below and the Golden Gate Bridge off in the distance. What a beautiful city. At that moment, I felt a stab of fear. What was I doing, leaving everything and everyone behind—my farm, my friends, and my family— a perfectly good life, in search of a dream?

Then tears of relief trickled down my cheeks. I was on my way. And Gilbert and his family waited for me there, my family, in France.

Darkness came early to a wet and cold "City of Light" in November. I had planned to spend a few days in Paris before heading west to Normandy to stay with Gilbert and Huguette. I found a youth hostel, a college dorm for visiting foreign students, which, at a fraction of the cost of a hotel, fit my budget. But being the age of everyone's mother and the reality of the tiny, dirty room weighed on my spirit.

Jet lag, some culture shock and realizing I didn't have an adapter for my computer added to my sense of stress and isolation.

This isn't how it is supposed to be. You should have the money to stay in a hotel and you should have bought the adapter before you left, the mean critical voice inside my head, which sounded just like my mother, informed me.

But I sensed that after a visit with Gilbert and Huguette and when I went south to Aix-en-Provence, a smaller city with a warmer climate, things would improve.

Late one afternoon, the search to find an adapter for my computer found me on a bus traveling through the darkening streets of Paris, headed to a strange part of the city. Jet lag kicked in each afternoon about four, and this day was no exception. I put my head against the bus window and took a breath, bracing myself for the sharp inner critic to chime in, berating me. Then I heard a new voice.

You're doing so great. I sat up and looked around, startled. Who was being so kind to me, and in English? The seat next to me was empty. It went on.

Look at you, you barely understand computers in English and now you're conversing about them in French. And traveling across Paris to an unfamiliar neighborhood, at night. You're amazing.

I looked out the window at the neon signs and buildings passing by in a blur and felt a sense of calm. Yes, I am being courageous, I thought. Thank you for noticing, whoever you are. In the midst of living on the edge, way beyond my comfort zone, had I found the "inner mother" I'd always been seeking—loving, accepting and encouraging?

I located the computer store, where the salesman thought I needed a $100 part. But he wasn't sure and something told me to wait. Then back across town on the bus to my familiar neighborhood near Boulevard Saint-Michel, where, to my relief, I recognized familiar storefronts and streets. As I got off the bus I spotted a tiny store with an Apple computer sign.

I ran up the stairs, out of the cold. An earnest-looking young man wearing black-rimmed spectacles stood at the counter. Behind him, computer parts protruded from every nook and cranny on messy shelves.

When I explained my dilemma he smiled a slight smile, possibly at my American accent. But he understood, turned and grabbed a little gizmo off the shelf, price tag, ten dollars. *Voilà!* My adapter. I skipped down the stairs and headed back to the hostel, smiling, remembering that voice and its sweet message.

Yes, I was doing so great.

The next few days felt like a roller coaster, high and excited one minute, then cold and lonely the next, especially in the chilly Paris evenings. I solved one part of the problem by investing in a long, black, wool coat that not only made me fit in like a Parisian, but kept me warm against the frigid winds blowing along Boulevard Saint-Germain.

One evening, on my way back to the hostel, something caught my eye in a shop window and I slowed down to look. Three words stood out against the backdrop of the window display.

"*Croyez-en-soi.*" Believe in yourself. I stopped and looked closer at the window—a bookstore, with textbooks, notebooks and school supplies. The words didn't seem to be related to anything in particular, but if there were any three words I needed at that moment, they were, *"Croyez-en-soi."*

Believing in myself meant trusting that I would find a home, friends, and a life in France for the next eight months. That I could trust myself, life, destiny—everything that had brought me to that exact moment, standing alone on a chilly corner in Paris, just weeks before the new millennium.

People bustled by, heading home with their fresh baguettes, cars honked and the wind blew golden leaves around the sidewalk. I stared at the words and let them sink in deep. If my eyes had been just a few inches higher or lower, if I had glanced away, I would have missed them.

But I didn't miss them. They would become my mantra as I stepped into my new life in France and from then on.

"Croyez-en-soi."

A few days later, I took the #21 bus across Paris to the Gare Saint-Lazare and caught the train to Normandy to visit Gilbert and Huguette. The comfort and familiarity of their warm home felt like a balm. We celebrated our two birthdays—Gilbert's and mine are only one day apart. They were excited that I was staying in France for eight months, giving us lots of chances to visit.

Gilbert liked to tease me, calling me *"notre petite Américaine,"* our little American. I take after my Dad and at almost five foot eleven, am a good four inches taller than Gilbert. I had to sleep at an angle in their guest bed and duck going up their wooden stairs to avoid bumping my head.

I knew that they were thrilled to see me each time I visited. My presence must have brought back memories of not only Dad, but also of all the good times we'd shared since our reunion. They had a video of their visit to California and we watched it together, laughing and remembering all of the special moments.

Huguette was worried that I was going south to a city where I knew no one and invited me to stay with them for my time in France. I considered her offer, but knew I needed to believe in myself and have the experience of finding my own way. I trusted that I was drawn to the south of France and Aix-en-Provence, so thanked her and reassured her that we could see each other and talk on the phone often.

I traveled back to Paris, then south on the train to Marseilles, to transfer to Aix-en-Provence. As the fast train sped south, rain spattered against the windows and clouds changed shape as the sky turned from gray to blue.

I snuggled up in my long, black wool coat and took a nap, waking up just as we pulled into Marseilles. I found the smaller, local train to Aix, then walked the fifteen minutes to my hotel, pulling my rolling bag.

Over the next few weeks, I discovered that finding an apartment was much harder than I had expected. In Aix, a university town, thousands of students had arrived months before, snagging all the best places. I called ad after ad from phone booths and looked at dark and dingy rooms above tattoo parlors, in basements, or on busy streets. Nothing felt right.

I wanted sunlight, windows and a bathtub—a place where I could write and feel renewed—and I wasn't going to settle for less. I was using up my resources staying in a hotel, but I had to trust and wait.

I found a group of British and American expatriates who met weekly for coffee and conversation. As much as I loved the challenge of speaking French, it was fun for that brief time to speak my native tongue.

A new French friend from the group Maïté, who came to practice her English, told me about an apartment in the old part of town, "*centre ville,*" a great location for walking to everything. She didn't know all the details, but gave me the phone number.

The next morning, the real estate agent and I met at the apartment and walked up the three flights of stairs, to the door on the left. The big rusty key turned in the lock and the door swung open to sunlight blazing through tall windows in the kitchen and living room. In the dining room, French doors opened to a tiny balcony. I turned the corner off the kitchen to the bathroom and saw a deep, old bathtub.

Sunlight, windows and a bathtub. I took a breath and smiled at the woman.

"I'll take it!" I said.

25

The apartment was partially furnished, meaning that it had furniture, but no towels, sheets or kitchen items. Maïté loaned me some kitchen things and drove me to a huge *supermarché*, where I bought sheets, towels and pillows. I put my new linens on the bed, hung the dishtowels in the kitchen, then took a long, hot soak in my bathtub, drying off with my fresh, new towels.

After heating some soup in my one saucepan, I put out the baguette, cheese and wine that I'd bought, set the table with my borrowed dishes and sat down for my first meal there. Then I snuggled into my cozy bed and drifted off to sleep. I was home. In France.

I left a few days later to take the train north to spend Christmas with Gilbert and Huguette. Storms had been raging all over France—the Seine was flooding in Paris and huge trees had fallen, stopping many trains. But my time in Normandy was quiet and sweet.

On Christmas Eve, Cathy and her sons came over to exchange gifts and we turned on the tiny tree in the window, with the bright colored lights. Huguette prepared a special feast of roast chicken and we sipped champagne and toasted the new millennium that was just days away. It felt so comforting to be "home for Christmas" with my family, in France.

As always, Huguette showed concern that I was all right in my life in the south, and told me again that I could come and stay with them for as long as I wanted or needed to. I reassured her that I was fine, especially now that I had found such a wonderful apartment.

Huguette's caring and concern reminded me a lot of my dad. Gilbert had found and married a woman who treated others with the same warmth and love as my father had. We planned for them to come and visit me in the spring and I was coming back to see them again in late January. They were my safety net, just a phone call and a train ride away.

I returned to Aix three days before the millennium, walking the short distance from the train station to my apartment and up the three flights of stairs. I stood at my front door, jiggling the key in the lock, just so, a little up and to the right and click, the old door creaked open. I peeked in, tentative at first—I'd heard that apartments got broken into a lot in France and I'd been gone for a week.

But it looked just as it had when I rushed out to catch the train to Paris. The hand-embroidered tablecloth I'd picked up at the open market for 28 francs, or four dollars, covered the weathered pine table. A slender purple iris, in a vase made of a blue glass juice bottle with the label soaked off, stood in the center. All was quiet.

I crept in, the cool tiles echoing my footsteps. My dishes drained on the counter in the new, white plastic dish drainer I'd bought just before I left. The cold air made me shiver, from no heat for a week and the frigid December nights and chilly mistral winds, which rattled the doors and windows.

But the late afternoon sunlight streamed in and reflected off the gold plastered walls and the orange floor tiles. As I moved around the corner to the bedroom to put down my suitcase, I let out the breath I didn't know I'd been holding.

Safe in my own apartment, I kept pinching myself. I was living in France, making a life, finding my way. With six months left of my adventure, what lay ahead? I felt breathless to find out.

As the new year unfolded, my days took on an easy rhythm. I walked to the open-air market to buy just-picked fruits and vegetables. The carrots tasted sweeter, the apples tart and the cherries more luscious than any I had ever known. The fruits that weren't grown locally came from Africa, reminding me how far I was from home. The large brown eggs, gathered from plump Provençal hens and displayed in a basket, still had downy feathers stuck to them.

In California, I had used an organizer for twenty years to plan my days. Here I relaxed and allowed the days to unfold. I learned to hang out. I spent whole afternoons at cafés with friends, where we engaged in spirited discussions, then went to a movie or dinner.

Other times, I sat alone and watched people or wrote, feasting my senses on the sound of water splashing in a fountain or sunlight slanting off a medieval building.

I appreciated the ritual of the more formal manners of the French. Entering the local bakery for my evening *baguette à l'ancienne*, an ancient recipe baguette, I was greeted warmly. Leaving, I traded salutations with the shopkeepers again, *Merci, bonsoir.* As I headed home to my apartment, the bread, still warm from the wood-fired oven, felt alive in my hands.

Walking everywhere kept me in shape, in spite of the croissants and *pain au chocolat* I consumed. Weekends, I hiked with my new friends up to the top of Mont Sainte-Victoire, the nearby peak painted by Cézanne, or along the jagged cliffs above the Mediterranean.

Life without a car felt carefree, unburdened by the hassles of parking, petrol, toll roads, or rental fees. I was able to go wherever I wanted by foot, bus, train or by hitching a ride with friends.

Aix was founded by the Romans because of a *source* or thermal spring. The site of the spring now was a spa, offering mud wraps, massages and baths at a reasonable price. I signed up for a series of treatments and went each week.

By February, the pure immersion of living in France for almost four months was paying off. I was at lunch at Maïté's and as everyone chattered in rapid French, I realized I could understand and respond, without thinking. Maïté congratulated me on my new ease and confidence in the language. I called Gilbert and Huguette often, never getting over the thrill of being in the same country and time zone.

I wrote and sold articles about my experiences living in France, including one to *More* magazine, entitled "My French Affaire, How I Did my Junior Year Abroad Thirty Years Late." It was a gift to have so much to write about and the time to do it.

In May, my daughter Michelle, her husband Claude and my nine-month-old granddaughter Ellie came over to visit. By then, I could switch back and forth from French to English like changing channels on the radio, a thrill that I'd waited almost forty years to achieve.

Gilbert and Huguette came and stayed during that time and we all enjoyed a special visit together. They applauded my apartment and how I'd settled in so well. I slept in the living room on a foldout couch and gave them my bedroom. It felt good to reciprocate their hospitality, in my own place, in France.

Just as I had mixed feelings when I arrived in France, I had similar feelings when it was time to return home. I had discovered a better quality of life there—my rent was lower, food was more reasonable and fresh, I lived without the expense of a car and savored the slower pace of life. I felt softer speaking French and reveled in the rhythm and elegance of the language.

In my eight-month stay, I discovered that I could create a life from nothing, in a foreign language and end up landing on my feet. My success in finding my sunny apartment, meeting great friends and my new fluency in French gave me a stronger and more certain sense of myself. I loved visiting Gilbert and Huguette and being more a part of their lives. But with my family and now a grandchild in America, I didn't want to be so far away.

Most importantly, as I looked back on my time in France, it felt like I had reached back in time and pulled that nineteen-year-old forward, reclaiming parts of myself at a deep level. I was grateful that I had been able to slow down, reevaluate my life and then come more into the present as I began the second half-century of my life.

The reality of taking apart my home in France was daunting. Maïté gave me a huge old suitcase to pack up as much as I could—antique linens, old dishes and crystal that had all been finds and I gave away the rest.

In Paris, I boarded my flight for the journey home. The next morning, in California, when I walked into a bakery and no one said *bonjour* or hello, I felt a pang of sadness.

My sister Sharon continued to struggle with her life and health challenges. The treatments had slowed down the growth of her brain tumors, but nothing, it seemed, was able to stop them. It was good that I went to France when I did. Once back home, I had to step in and help her more and more as time went on.

The sister I'd known and loved for my whole life was slipping away. I lost her month by month as we passed milestones.

First she was unable to manage her money, then unable to live alone, then unable to walk, then unable to get out of bed. The grief of it hit me each time we reached a new, sad milestone.

Two-and-a-half years after my return, my sister died at home, surrounded by her children, family and a few close friends. Sharon's battle was over, but I struggled with the reality that she was gone. She had not only been my sister, but played the role of the loving and nurturing mother I never had.

I had kept in touch with Gilbert and Huguette throughout Sharon's illness and Huguette and I cried together when I told her about Sharon's death. I'd been so caught up in helping my sister that I'd not been able to visit them since returning from France in 2000. The 60th anniversary of D-Day was coming up the next year in June 2004. I set a goal to go.

On a whim, I contacted Stephen Ambrose Historical Tours to see if they needed any tour guides or translators for their anniversary tours. I sent them my articles and qualifications and they called me back and said yes, I was hired.

I would accompany a group of army U.S. Army Rangers in France for the anniversary. I was thrilled. I made arrangements to go a week early to spend time with Gilbert and Huguette before the tour began and also to have some time to visit with them again after.

With my trip lined up, on another hunch, I sent a proposal to the local National Public Radio station about doing a series of commentaries for the upcoming anniversary. The manager of the station called me right back, excited. "You have no idea how rare it is to have something of this quality come across my desk," he said. Another chance to be thrilled.

In the months before my trip, I traveled to the Seabee Museum and archives at Point Mugu Naval Base, north of Los Angeles, hoping to gather some new information about Dad's time in France. After getting a security clearance to come onto the base, I sat down in a room with seven large cardboard filing boxes of artifacts from my father's battalion, the 111th Seabee Naval Construction Battalion, from 1943-1945.

For hours, on the first morning, I sifted through the boxes of papers, disappointed to find nothing related to Dad. Then I saw some neat fine printing from a report of the "officer of the day." At the end of it was my father's signature, *Lieutenant Donald K. Johnson.* I held the paper close to my heart, knowing that Dad had signed it sixty years before.

In the next box, I came across a grainy black-and-white photo of a group of sailors lined up in a field in Normandy. Dad stood straight and tall at one end, in his officer's uniform and hat. He was not smiling.

What was he thinking and feeling that day? Was that photo taken near the end, when Dad knew that he couldn't bring Gilbert home with him? Was Gilbert waiting at the side, just outside of the photograph, for Dad to finish? I so wished I could have jumped into the scene and followed him around and asked him all the questions that I now knew to ask.

There were photos of the tents, lined up in neat rows, in the camp on the cliff above Omaha Beach. In another photo, men sat in a field attending Catholic Mass, the priest in front in his long robes. I searched in the crowd for Dad, but didn't find him there.

I found papers listing different projects that Dad had worked on in the surrounding areas. He and his team spent over a week in Bayeux, doing some restoration. I learned that Dad had been one of the officers in charge of building the Rhino Ferries in England in the months leading up to the invasion and learned more about the important part the ferries, called "a secret weapon of the invasion," played on D-Day and beyond.

I saw the hand-written lists of assignments for the D-Day invasion, with my father's name, then "D-Day plus one,"

Omaha Beach. I took in a quick breath, knowing again the good fortune that gave him the orders to land the day after D-Day on "Bloody Omaha."

As I sat in the room surrounded by the dusty boxes and papers of my father's battalion, I could feel him there, in France, in the life he had before I was born, the life that included Gilbert, who had now been my French brother for almost ten years.

26

I arrived in Paris and took the train from Gare Saint-Lazare to Normandy, a journey I had made so many times before, to visit Gilbert and Huguette. As always, when the train pulled into the station in Caen, Gilbert waited in the crowd to meet me. He waved and smiled, giving me the special four kisses of welcome, then pulled my bag along to their car.

"*Ça va Diane?*" he asked. Everything going well?

Back at their cozy home, we shared the warm meal that Huguette had prepared, then they shooed me off to bed to rest and recover from my jet lag. We spent the next relaxing days together enjoying Huguette's delicious food and catching up on the time that had passed since our last visit together in France in 2000. At the end, I felt rested and ready for the upcoming tour.

All of Normandy hummed with excitement for the big anniversary. It would be the last one that many of the veterans, now in their late seventies and early eighties, would be able to attend. The presidents of America and France and the Chancellor of Germany would all attend the formal ceremony on June 6th at the American cemetery at Colleville-sur-Mer.

After my time with Gilbert, I returned to Paris, rounded up my sweet veterans and their families at the airport and we all boarded the bus to head back to Normandy. My group, seven members of the elite Army Rangers, had scaled the one-hundred-foot cliff, Pointe du Hoc, on the morning of D-Day, straight up into the fury of the Germans.

I did some research on the Rangers and felt in awe of what they faced and overcame on D-Day. As they scaled the cliff, the Germans at the top shot down at them, cut their ropes, threw back their ladders and dropped grenades and boulders down on them. Of the two-hundred-forty Rangers who began the ascent up the cliff, one-hundred-eighty made it to the top to face hand-to-hand combat.

They defeated those Germans, then, found and destroyed five big enemy guns that were pounding the beaches below. That act alone saved thousands of American lives on D-Day and beyond. By the time the Rangers were relieved two days later, ninety-one had been killed and fifty-nine wounded. Ninety were able to continue to fight. D-day and the days following, the residents of the nearby villages welcomed the Rangers with open arms. They shared food and champagne, but especially their gratitude.

These same villages have never stopped welcoming returning Rangers through the years. Of the seven Rangers returning for the 60th anniversary, one man had returned with family members every five years, though most had not been back since 1944.

When we arrived in Normandy, French and American flags hung from windows everywhere. People stopped and waved when our bus, with the words "American Army Rangers" on the side, went by.

The villagers treated the veterans like honored guests. At one small ceremony in a village square, the French and American national anthems alternated, playing out of a tinny sound system set up in a van. But you could feel the heart that went into all the preparations. The French and the veterans were grateful for my translation and we'd stand together, moved and touched, wiping away tears.

Our group attended a special mass in the first village liberated by the Rangers in 1944. All ages, from tiny children to elderly grandparents, crowded into the church and stood up in respect when we walked in.

The elders had passed the stories down to their children and grandchildren, telling about the brave young men who landed and saved them on that June morning sixty years before. Afterwards, we sipped champagne and ate sweet butter cookies together outside on the lawn.

The veterans jumped right into the celebrations, shaking hands, signing autographs and posing for photos. The sun was hot, the hours were long, the jet lag was hard, but they were in their glory and everyone wanted them to have it.

One of the French hosts spoke for many of the villagers when welcoming the veterans:

"Here in Normandy, we don't forget the heroes who liberated us in the last war, and those who died here. Here in Normandy, we will never forget."

On the afternoon of June 6th, the Army had arranged a special ceremony just for the Rangers. At this intimate and powerful event, the seven men stood at attention, saluting. Their shoulders were stooped with age; they couldn't stand as straight and tall as they had all those years before. But you could see the pride in the way they held themselves. You could see the soldiers they had been.

Afterwards, young army men and women thronged around to listen to them, to shake their hands and to be photographed with them. The veterans were being rightfully honored as the heroes that they were.

The next day I skipped a boat outing to the cliffs at Pointe du Hoc in order to call the National Public Radio station for an interview. As I left the phone booth, I noticed my group of veterans and their families frantically waving their arms and yelling at me across the harbor. Something was clearly wrong.

As I gazed across the water between us, I realized I couldn't get to them without going around and it was way too far to walk or run. Starting to feel panicked myself, I flagged down a passing truck and asked if they could please drive me to the other side of the harbor. We sped over to the group.

One of the veterans, Ivor, normally outgoing and energetic, lay unmoving in an ambulance. His son, who had traveled with him to the reunion, was in tears, helpless and unable to understand what was going on.

I sorted out that Ivor had had a stroke and that the paramedics were taking him to Bayeux, the closest hospital. A local offered to drive us, so we hopped into his car and followed the ambulance. No one at the hospital spoke English, so I agreed to help until Ivor could be transferred to the American hospital in Paris where more of the staff spoke English.

It took three days to arrange the transfer and to make sure that Ivor was strong enough to make the drive to Paris in the ambulance. At the American hospital, he could rest and heal until he was able to withstand the long flight home.

He'd told his son over and over, "I just want to make it back to Normandy for the anniversary and reunion." He'd gotten his wish, but unfortunately, the day after, had a stroke. His son and I shook our heads at the irony of that. The day that they left for Paris, I stood by the ambulance to say goodbye and his son took my hands.

"Your father would have been so proud of you," he said. We both wiped away tears as we hugged goodbye.

After several more weeks in the hospital in Paris, Ivor

healed enough to travel home. He lived another year before his son called to tell me that his father had died. The sixtieth anniversary and reunion had been one of the high points of his father's life and he had relived the pleasure of it over and over during his last months.

Helping them had been one of the most rewarding and moving experiences of my life and showed me, once again, the power of a language to bridge worlds. Gilbert picked me up for a short visit before I headed back to Paris and home and I shared with them many of my memories from the tour.

Being with the veterans and their families and witnessing the gratitude of the French towards the *vieux soldats*, the old soldiers, gave me another experience of my father's generation, whom Tom Brokaw called "The Greatest Generation." Here are the closing words of my final National Public Radio commentary recorded from the Paris N.P.R. office and sent back to the California station:

"My father's stories about the Normandy Invasion were not about war, per se, but about relationships. Sixty years later, I too will be telling stories about the relationships I experienced in Normandy, between the veterans and their families, between the young and the old, between the French and the Americans.

Everyone has gone home now. The returning travelers will have stories to tell at their Veterans of Foreign War meetings. Their long-time friends will lean in close, hands cupped over their ears, to catch all the details of the powerful journey.

For the rest of us who were on the trip, we'll never forget that we were there with them, that one last time.

I think we're fascinated with World War II because it was a display of courage by so many ordinary men. In the face of danger and death, they did the right thing. Not only the right thing, the heroic thing.

I think we're fascinated with the story because we want to believe that we all have the capacity within us to be heroes, to be great, to be courageous, even in the face of death.

WWII veterans are dying at the rate of one thousand per day. While they're still here with us, we have the chance to ask them questions and to listen. To thank them. They gave us so much. Now it's our turn to give back to them.

And if you look into their eyes, you can see who they were. It's right there. You just have to look."

27

Gilbert and Huguette put my mother on a pedestal, calling her *Mamie Bonnye*, Grandmother Bonnye. My mother liked to be called "Nana Bonnye" in America, but the word "nana" in French has some kind of a "fast chick" connotation.

Huguette's mother had died and my mother was the closest thing Gilbert had to a mother, so they treated Mom with respect and love. That may have helped my mother, to have someone consider her special like that.

Mom was not a warm person, but with my interpreting back and forth, both in person and in letters, she came across as warm enough. I helped Mom to write cards for Christmas and birthdays and Gilbert and Huguette always asked about her when we talked on the phone.

After my sister died, I needed some time away from our small town; I felt haunted by Sharon's memory everywhere I turned. Fourteen years had passed since I had moved to Northern California and I thought I'd try living in Southern California again, nearer to my daughters.

I rented out my house in Nevada City and found a studio near the beach, an hour from my daughters and grandchildren and twenty minutes from my mother. I was able to spend precious time with my granddaughters who were then two and four, and to see my daughters more often.

Of course, living that close to my mother brought up all that was unhealed in my relationship with her, a real challenge. When my N.P.R. commentaries were going to air about the 60th anniversary of D-Day, I went over to my mother's house, set up the radio on the right station and wrote down the times for her.

I was so excited to share this with her, to show her real evidence of the place I was making for myself in the world. But somehow she couldn't make the time to listen. Each time, she forgot. When I received an award for the commentaries, she barely acknowledged my success. She was in her late eighties. She was not going to change.

We both were missing my sister Sharon, but Sharon's death, if anything, made her even more of a saint to my mother. "Sharon would not have eaten the last banana," my mother snapped at me one day. Clearly, if there was going to be any healing in this last chapter of our lives together, it would have to be initiated by me.

One of my spiritual teachers, the late Irish poet and philosopher John O'Donohue, gave me some advice. He said, "Just be kind to your mother; she's old and you're not." His suggestion intrigued me. It bypassed all our history and demanded that I take the high road, no matter what she did.

I followed his advice, painful as it was in the face of her criticism or indifference. I started coming over on Sundays, bringing groceries and fixing dinner for her. I baked her scones and froze them so she could take one out each night and have it for her breakfast the next day.

I went with her to her doctor's appointments and made sure that they were doing all that they could for her. I rubbed thick cream on the dry, scabby skin on her legs and arms at night before I tucked her into bed.

I "mothered" her in ways that she had never been able to

mother me. "Just be kind to her; she's old and you're not," became my own personal mantra. Sometimes I gritted my teeth and took deep breaths in order to not react in anger. But over time, being kind to her created some peace and healing.

At ninety-one, Mom was still healthy, but her lungs were failing. She went into a rehabilitation hospital for special treatments, but after a month, nothing was helping. I visited her most nights after I completed my workday of life coaching and writing. She sometimes called me as many as three times a day, asking me to do things.

One night, I rushed over and took care of what she had wanted: to talk to the nurses about her lung treatments, to get her a cup of hot coffee and to go to her condo for her special thick Australian wool blanket. By eight o'clock, I felt exhausted and was feeling resentful that she, as usual, hadn't thanked me for my efforts. I thought I'd try something new and ask her to thank me.

So I took a deep breath and said, "Mom, I'm hungry and tired and need to go. It would mean a lot if you thanked me for rushing over here and doing all the things you wanted." She looked at me, maybe a little startled, and didn't say anything for a moment.

Then she said, "Thank you for everything you did for me tonight." I felt some warmth in that and was grateful. I gave her a kiss and said goodnight. As I walked out the door, I turned back and looked at her. She looked open, even vulnerable and there was a softness to her countenance that I hadn't seen before. It felt like an opening. I paused and almost went back in to give her another hug. But I didn't. I so wish I had.

The next day, I attended a special luncheon in Los Angeles and made the two-hour drive each way. During the lunch, I felt a sense of urgency, like my mother was not doing well and kept checking my cell phone, which didn't ring. It was all very subtle, but I noticed myself thinking, *Hold on. Just a little longer, Mom.*

On the drive back, one of my brothers called and announced that they planned to move Mom to Los Angeles. I told him that she would hate that change so late in her life, but he was insistent. Mom had always told me that she had spirit guides around her, so I started talking to her in my head.

Mom, it's time to go. You're ninety-one years old and have had a good life. Have your spirit guides help you to let go now. It's time.

Fifteen minutes later, I walked into the hospital lobby and signed in. The woman behind the counter recognized me. "Ms. Covington, your mother…"

"Just let me go up to her," I said, running towards the elevator.

Out of the elevator and past the nurse's station, the same scenario, "Ms. Covington, your mother…"

I ran past them and into her room. The oxygen machine made a whooshing sound, but under the mask, she lay completely still. She was gone. The nurse was right behind me.

"Get that thing off of her face, now," I barked. The nurse took it off.

"Is there anything we can do for you?" she asked.

"Yes, I'd like to sit with her and I'd like a drink of water," I said. The nurse closed the curtain around Mom's bed with a swish, then returned, moments later, with water in a paper cup.

"Thank you," I said.

I touched my mother's chest. It was still warm but she wasn't breathing. I held her hand and noticed her bright orange nail polish. She'd just had her nails done a few days before as a special treat. I put my head down on her chest and cried quiet tears.

This was my mother. This was the body that brought me into the world. The drama between us was now over. It was time to say goodbye.

I called Mom's church and asked the priest to come to say last rites before they took her body away. My Catholic training taught me that praying for someone right after they die, can help their soul. That night I went to a twenty-four hour chapel and prayed and the next morning went to mass for her.

At her memorial service later that week, I requested that we sing the hymn that I sang with her when I was eight, "Everlasting is Thy Reign." As we sang it in her memory, I could still hear her voice in my head, with her accent, as she had sounded all those years before.

She was gone. But I was grateful that we had a chance to be different with each other before the end. It wasn't the loving and warm relationship I had longed for, but it wasn't raging and angry either. There had been some healing. I had been able to be kind. I called Gilbert and Huguette to tell them about Mom's death and Huguette cried. They'd hoped to somehow see her one more time.

After my mother died, I moved back home to Nevada City, happy to be back at my farm with the peace and space that it provided. My mother left behind some money and I began to do some much-needed maintenance—clearing out brush down at the creek, planting new trees, tearing down a shed, building a deck, painting and cleaning.

It felt "grand" as Dad liked to say. At the end of the summer, I looked forward to the magic of the seasons again, the subtle changes that signaled summer turning into fall.

I felt liberated, knowing that the struggle with my mother was over. I'd done my best to try to heal with her and now felt energized to begin a new chapter in my life. The money from Mom also gave me some time and space to draw back from working and to slow down. I could devote more time and energy to writing.

I could return to France.

28

Fall 2007, I began planning a month-long trip to France for February 2008, setting up various assignments for articles. At the beginning of the trip, I set aside time to visit Gilbert and Huguette for a long visit. I hadn't been back since 2004 and looked forward to spending time with them again.

In October, Huguette expressed concern that Gilbert had lost a lot of weight and he was going to have some tests to see if they could find out the cause. He was so healthy. Surely nothing could be wrong.

In November, Huguette called to tell me that Gilbert had been diagnosed with liver cancer. With treatment and rest, they felt hopeful that he could fight the disease. Huguette was retired and could take care of him. We talked on the phone often for updates but as the weeks passed, the news wasn't good; he was failing fast. I hoped and prayed that I could get there in time.

Hold on, I thought, as I packed and completed things for my upcoming trip. *I'm coming. Just a few more days now.* Sharon had held on for years; I prayed that Gilbert could last a few more weeks.

"Diane will be here soon," Huguette told him and he smiled and seemed comforted.

But he couldn't hold on. He died two weeks before I was

scheduled to leave for France. Huguette and I cried together when she told me the news. After the phone call, I sat at my desk and stared out the window at the gray January sky, then called Huguette right back to find out the plans for the memorial.

As we spoke again, I knew it was completely unreasonable and maybe impossible, but I had to try to get there in time for his funeral. After a flurry of phone calls and condensing two weeks into a few hours, I left to drive to San Francisco to catch the next day's flight to Paris. If I traveled straight through, I might just make it.

The next afternoon, I settled into my seat on Air France for the long flight across the Atlantic. As we flew into the night, I felt grateful for the quiet as the other passengers slept all around me. But I couldn't sleep. After the shock of the news and all the rushing to leave, it was my first chance to stop and gather my thoughts.

I was on my way to Gilbert's funeral. The story that began almost sixty-four years before was now complete. Gilbert and my dad were both gone. And yet here I was, with my heart tangled up too, compelled to be there for Gilbert's funeral. Was that for me, or for my dad?

I didn't know, I only knew that I trusted the mysteries of life and death and love that were pushing me through the night sky, toward France. I let the warm tears fall, grateful that in the darkness, no one could see. The huge jet engines droned and finally, I slept.

The next morning in Paris, I took the R.E.R. train into the city and then the Metro to the Gare Saint-Lazare, to catch the train to Normandy. As soon as I bought my ticket, I called Huguette to tell her when I was arriving. I napped during the two-hour journey, my head against the cold glass of the rattling train window, as it passed through the colorless winter landscape.

When I stepped off the train in Caen, I started searching the faces of the crowd, looking for Gilbert. Then I remembered. Gilbert won't be coming this time, or ever again, to meet me at the train. It felt so sad, so final.

I spotted Cathy, their daughter, in the crowd. We exchanged kisses, then looked at each other and both started to cry. People don't hug in France the way we do in America, but we hugged each other, standing there in the train station in Caen on that cold winter evening, with people rushing past all around us.

At their house, Huguette greeted me warmly. She'd fixed me a delicious soup and after a bowl, I went straight up to what felt like "my room," the guest room, to sleep. I'd been traveling almost twenty-four hours, but I had made it. I had arrived in time for the funeral.

The next morning, the family gathered at the mortuary to sit with Gilbert's body for the last time. He looked frail and thin, lying in the casket, not like his usual robust and exuberant self, but I said goodbye to the physical form that had carried his heart and soul.

I remembered how I had sat with the bodies of my father, my sister and then my mother, such a powerful wake-up call to the preciousness of life. I wished I'd been able to come back to visit sooner. But it felt intimate and deep to be in the inner circle of the family as we sat with Gilbert's body and grieved his loss.

The word "family" could be defined as the people you share your joys and your sorrows with, I realized. Sometimes you're related to them by blood and sometimes you're not. That day, as I sat with them in the small room at the mortuary, saying goodbye to Gilbert, I knew I was their family and they were mine.

In Gilbert's tiny village, bells tolled as relatives and friends braved the chilly, gray day to gather at the church for his funeral.

We waited outside as an honor guard of fellow veterans carried his coffin, draped by the tricolor French flag, into the church.

My breath came out in clouds and I shivered down into my thick wool coat. As I reached up to pull my scarf tighter, I happened to feel the pulse in my neck, steady and strong, *thump, thump, thump,* such a reminder that I was alive and well on that freezing morning that I was saying goodbye to my French brother.

I sat in the front pew between Huguette and Cathy. During the service, the priest asked me to place a photo of my father and one of Gilbert from 1944, together in one frame, on the coffin. There was a slight murmur as I did that— everyone in the packed church knew the story. I felt honored to be a part of the service and to have Dad remembered at that moment too.

They played a Celine Dion song, *"S'il Suffisait d'Aimer,"* "If it is Enough to Love." I remembered playing that song for Gilbert and Huguette when they visited me in Aix-en-Provence. As I let in the music and the words, I thought, Yes, it is enough to love. It is more than enough. It is everything.

The priest spoke about Gilbert's life and as I listened to the words honoring him, I realized again that if Gilbert had become my American brother, the story would have ended there. Instead, over six decades later, I sat as part of Gilbert's family, in his village in France.

Candlelight flickered on the faces of the handsome young Naval officer and the sweet little boy as we prayed, sang and sat in silence.

Cathy had been right. It was *le destin* that my father and Gilbert had loved each other and then had to say goodbye. As the music echoed off the walls of the old church, I knew it had also been my destiny, linked by their love across space and time, to bring them back together.

After the church service, the family returned to the funeral home. We sat in a small room with Gilbert's coffin, the man in charge said a few words, then the coffin moved away on a track, through some doors, toward being cremated. The cultural anthropologist in me found this difference from America interesting, though a little startling. It seemed to draw out the process of saying goodbye and Huguette was weeping. But there was also a finality, when those doors closed, that he was gone forever.

Close friends and family gathered back at the house for a luncheon. Extra leaves expanded the dining table and everyone crowded around. I was so grateful for my ability to understand the chatter of the conversation and to participate. I even told the story about how Dad's French teacher made "*s'il vous plaît*" sound like "silver plate." They all laughed. I'd never told a story in French before and gotten a laugh.

Huguette struggled with the emptiness and grief of losing Gilbert, her husband of almost fifty years. My presence seemed to comfort her and it gave her daughter Cathy a little breather, so I stayed five more days. We visited the cemetery each day, and went to a special mass for Gilbert. At home, we ate her delicious food and rested.

The day that I left, Huguette and her grandson Romain drove me to the train station in Caen. Romain had been a boy of twelve when they visited California; now he was twenty-three. We shivered together in the February cold as we waited on the platform.

When the train screeched to a halt, Romain hefted my bag up for me and Huguette waved and blew kisses as the train pulled away. I waved until I couldn't see them any more, wiping away tears and trying to compose myself as the train rattled down the tracks and headed back to Paris.

I left knowing that losing someone you care about is the same in any language. And with Gilbert and my father both gone, that chapter of the story was over. But the light of the love that they shared lived on, in me, in Huguette and in everyone who knew the story.

I arrived back in Paris and took the #21 bus across town to my hotel in the Latin Quarter and spent the chilly, rainy day walking the streets of Paris. At Notre Dame Cathedral, I prayed and lit a candle for Gilbert and all the loved ones I'd lost. The quiet and reverence of the ancient cathedral soothed and calmed me. The sun came out around sunset, lighting up the bridges crossing the Seine as I hurried back to my hotel.

A few days later, I began my planned itinerary, which included seawater spa treatments in La Baule, a truffle hunt in the Dordogne and then on to my beloved Aix-en-Provence. Near the end of the trip, I arrived in Aix late at night at the old train station and for a moment, couldn't remember which way to walk to get to the *centre ville*, the center of town.

Someone pointed out the way and after five minutes, I felt the relief of seeing the main street, Cours Mirabeau with its giant fountain. I checked into my hotel, feeling safe and secure in my "home town" in France once again.

The next few days, as I walked around Aix, reconnecting with Maïté and other old friends, it felt like I'd never left, though I'd been gone almost eight years. As I was buying some apples at the open market, talking to the farmer and exchanging pleasantries, I felt a moment of pure happiness and contentment.

How mysterious happiness is. It comes in little spurts that always feel like a gift, even a surprise. They're unpredictable and erratic, but so welcome. After the sadness of losing Gilbert, the moment felt like a balm.

I saw how being in France and speaking French, the language of my soul, made me happy, another mystery. I decided at that moment that I was not going to question any more the why or wherefore of happiness. I was going to enjoy it and count the blessings of it, wherever they came from.

29

Back in California, at my beloved farm, I kept the huge rock fireplace going day and night, cozy and warm against the late February snow and rain. As winter turned to spring, the old apple trees burst into bloom once again with delicate pink-and-white blossoms, the bees buzzed merrily and it looked like it was going to be a good year for apples.

The rebirth of spring, the warmth and beauty of new life after the dark and cold winter, felt especially powerful this year. Then summer, a big garden, a flock of hens raised from fuzzy chicks and the bounty of tomatoes, squash, berries and greens. My daughters and their families came to visit and life felt rich and good.

Since my divorce at age thirty, I'd relished having the freedom to follow my dreams, to have the experience of being "fiercely independent." I had lived in France, traveled to India twice and begun to establish myself as a writer. My daughters were now married and doing well, I had three beautiful grandchildren, good friends and work that I loved. I cherished my life and my home on my little farm.

Yet I longed to find a true partner, someone I could commit to and share my life with. In my years of being single, I'd had some powerful and healing relationships, but had not felt ready to make a long-term commitment. Now my journey through life alone felt complete.

I felt ready to be more open and vulnerable. I had a close friend, a psychiatrist, who said to me once, "You're going to find your partner. You had a good relationship with your father. It will happen." Those words comforted me and I hoped they were true.

In the beginning of 2009, a psychic told me that I would find "big love" by the fall. Could that really be possible? I decided to prepare for it and be ready, just in case. I cleaned and cleared and made room for someone, both in my house and in my mind.

As I was writing in my journal, I thought of Landon Carter, whom I'd met thirty years before when he led my "Six-day training." I'd never forgotten how dynamic he was and how, at that time, I thought he was my "ideal man."

I decided to follow a hunch and try to contact him to thank him for the difference he made in my life all those years before. I found him on the Internet and sent him an email.

When I looked at his photo on his website, I felt a tug of tenderness at my heart. He looked kind of vulnerable, as if he hadn't had the easiest time. But he still looked open and present, qualities that I'd so admired in him before. I noticed that he lived in New Zealand. How much farther away can you get and still be on this planet? I thought.

He answered my email and from that first moment, I felt a rapport and a connection between us. I ordered a book he'd written and began to read it. At the end of the summer, I came across the book again and wrote him another email to tell him that I had some ideas to make his book more powerful and more reflective of his dynamic personality. He was staying in San Francisco, a few hours away, so we arranged to get together.

Landon drove up to meet me at the farm in late October.

As we spent time together discussing his book, I knew that he was the kind of man I'd been waiting for. We shared similar interests and deep values—personal growth, travel, writing, and a love of nature.

He came back and spent the next weekend with me and we had a powerful, romantic and relaxing time together, going to the river near my home, being cozy by the fire and sleeping out on my deck, under the stars.

But we faced some major obstacles. For one, he lived in New Zealand, and I lived in California, a fact that gave new meaning to the term "long-distance relationship." And though he was also looking for a partner, and we had an amazing connection, he wasn't as interested in me as I was in him.

In the months ahead, as Landon traveled between New Zealand and California and I journeyed to New Zealand, we navigated the stormy waters of our on-again, off-again long-distance relationship.

But because we'd both been on a path of personal growth most of our lives, we agreed to base our relationship on telling the truth as we worked to sort out whether we were meant to be partners. In the process, we created a strong, solid relationship based on reality and not on fantasy. He moved in with me at my farm seven months later.

A year later, we traveled to France and visited Huguette. She'd known me by myself for our whole friendship, seventeen years. Landon doesn't speak French, was jet-lagged and a bit grumpy, and Huguette seemed cautious.

"*Est-ce-qu'il est gentil avec toi?*" she asked. Is he kind to you?

I told her we'd had some challenges at the beginning, but reassured her that yes, he was kind to me. She nodded and relaxed.

Huguette still struggled without Gilbert, but she now had a great-grandson, Tim, Romain's son, who gave her a new purpose and lots of joy. As I watched her cuddle Tim, I could imagine her telling him the story of his great-grandfather, Gilbert, who almost went to America as a boy and the American family that lives across the ocean.

Someday, Tim might become interested in learning English and traveling to America to meet these relatives. It's a mystery what part *le destin* will play in this story.

After our visit with Huguette, Landon and I took the train to Annecy, the beautiful lake town that I'd visited in 1982, almost thirty years before. We stayed two weeks, swimming in the crystal-clear water, bicycling around the lake and savoring the rich experience of the food, culture and language. I relished fulfilling my dream to return to Annecy, this time with my long-awaited partner.

Landon and I were married the following year, surrounded by family and friends at the farm, on a warm summer day. Our grandchildren carried baskets of flowers and my daughters were my bridesmaids as Landon and I celebrated our commitment to each other and to our future together.

We danced our first dance to the old song "At Last My Love Has Come Along" as friends and family swayed with us. The day was perfect. I sent Huguette a photo album of our wedding to share our joy.

In my new life, Landon and I travel between New Zealand and California, enjoying the beauty of both places. We plan to visit France again and, of course, Huguette.

I look forward to the continued unfolding of the story, through the years and across time and space.

The story and the love will live on.

Epilogue

As I write this, I am preparing to journey to France in June 2014 for the 70th anniversary of D-Day. I will be traveling again with Stephen Ambrose Historical Tours as a guide and translator between the veterans and the French. Huguette and I will be able to spend time together again.

Twenty-one years ago, in 1993, when I traveled to France to research the essay for the upcoming 50th anniversary of D-Day, I had no idea the stream of events that would be set in motion by that essay, and how, all linked together, they would lead me to Gilbert.

It's easy to see, looking back, the fragility of all those connections and to feel the wonder and gratitude of how it came together. This was all before cellphones and email—any "misses" would have been fatal.

The late John O'Donohue talked about how we're being "minded" in our lives, guided by unseen hands. Looking back over six decades of life, I know that he is right. I don't understand the mystery of it, but I can see all the times and places where that has been true in my life.

For all of the years that I was pulled back to studying French, I had no way to explain the wonder the language held for me and still holds for me. The joy I feel when I speak it, the pleasurable sensation of my brain remembering which sounds to make when, the miracle of being understood.

From the first moment I heard *chambre meublée* when I was twelve years old, I could feel another life calling out to me and pulling me towards it.

I know now, more than ever, that we have to trust our hunches and urgings. We have to believe in ourselves, in our passions and dreams and in the difference that our unique lives can make. I know now that those dreams open a doorway to our destinies.

My father was a storyteller. He passed that down to me. Maybe that is why I've been compelled to be a writer, to be the "keeper of the stories" in my family and in my life.

I hope that this story will remind others of the power of love and kindness and even of the power of stories to soothe and calm us.

We're here to love and be loved. Everything else is like cotton candy—it looks pretty, but then you discover that there is no real substance to it, no real nourishment there.

Someone said, "In the end, it's all about who you love and letting them know." That is true. I know that now.

I wish you blessings on your lives and on your stories of love.

May they bring you, and those around you, great joy.

Diane Covington-Carter
Nevada City, California,
April 2014

Acknowledgements

To all the members of my writing circle, who listened as this work distilled itself into words on the page, week after week, month after month.

To my Writing Angels, Marilee Ford, Susan Prilliman, Heather Williams and Landon Carter, who read my final draft to help me to know if I was done.

To Sands Hall, writer and editor extraordinaire, who helped me to polish the story for *Reader's Digest*, which then propelled me to write the book. Also Christine Hemp and Maria Polglase Clement, who provided invaluable professional editing and encouragement.

To the press attaché at the French Consulate, Chantal Haag, who encouraged me to place the ad to find Gilbert.

To my dear friend, Maïté le Dantec, who checked my French to make sure it was correct.

To Tom Milam, for getting me to France in 1993 so that I could write that first essay.

To Margaret Jean Campbell for patient and tireless help with cover design, layout, and all things techincal.

To all the readers of the essay published in the *Reader's Digest* who tracked me down to tell me how much the story meant to them.

To Stephen Ambrose Historical Tours, for hiring me as a guide and translator for the 60th and 70th anniversaries of D-Day, giving me such rich chances to immerse myself in the history and reality of the Normandy Invasion.

To my daughters, Michelle and Heather, for being on the journey of life with me.

And finally, to my husband, Landon Carter, for his unfailing patience, love and support as I struggled in the deep and powerful work necessary to complete this book. The space he held for me made all the difference.

Author's note

In addition to my father's stories, I have read countless books on the Normandy Invasion and World War II and have learned a lot by participating in the D-Day anniversary celebrations in France.

I owe thanks to the many veterans who have told their stories on websites, describing in detail the scene on Omaha Beach, when they landed on D-Day, the bodies, the sea red with the blood of the dead young men, their own horror, pain and struggles to survive. Also, movies such as *Saving Private Ryan* and *The Longest Day* have portrayed the invasion in realistic detail.

In 2004, Captain Bill Hilderbrand, Civil Engineer Corps, U.S. Navy (Retired), President of the C.E.C./Seabee Historical Foundation, gave me a list of survivors from Dad's 111th Seabee battalion, which allowed me the chance to talk to both officers and enlisted men.

One of the sailors, William (Bill) Rostich, remembered Dad and his relationship with Gilbert, and provided me with valuable information that allowed me to piece together more details for some of the scenes for this book.

Rostich told me about the baseball games in the evening and also remembered that Dad made Gilbert take a shower, during which Gilbert howled. Knowing my father, I guessed that there was a reason for that shower, besides Dad loving for his children to be clean.

It would have been so much like my father to buy Gilbert some new clothes to have after Dad left, to remember him by, as Dad did for me before we parted when I was eighteen.

At the Seabee museum in Port Hueneme, California, I had access to all the records from Dad's battalion from 1943-1945. I read papers documenting how Dad and his team went back and forth to Bayeux for a week for a restoration project and knew that the village had not been destroyed during the invasion, meaning Dad would have had access to shops during that time. I was not able to verify this fact with Gilbert however before he died, so need to be forgiven for possible artistic license in that scene about the clothes.

My research at the Seabee museum was also so helpful in providing facts about Dad's experience in Normandy. For example, I read the hand-written list of assignments for D-Day, with my father's team going in on D-Day plus 1 and saw when Dad's duties included being "the officer of the day."

That research and those boxes of papers gave me a more complete picture of life in France during my father's time there, but also details that helped to fill out the story. I saw the exact date that Dad left Normandy in late October, for example, telling me how long Dad and Gilbert were together, almost five months. I saw photos of the evening baseball and football games and other rare photos of Dad and his men.

Dad's military records, which I was able to obtain as a family member, also helped to fill in details. That's where I learned that he was one of the officers in charge of building the Rhino Ferries. Dad was not one to draw attention to himself or to brag. He also never mentioned the fact that he had won a medal for sharpshooting during his training or been a champion boxer in college, details which came from his military records.

I also learned a lot from reading my parents' letters from that time. My father pleaded with my mother to write more.

She was busy going to dances, which created tension with my father's parents, with whom she was staying on their farm. They would have been babysitting my two older brothers, Clark and Kenton, one and three when my mother went out dancing.

In writing a story like this, the facts create the structure, which needs to be filled out with details that can't always be verified. I so wish I had asked a million more questions before my father and Gilbert died. So, for example, I'm not sure of the exact menu that the navy camp served at lunch and dinner. I had to guess based on the typical American diet, meat and potatoes, during that time period.

I did learn that the Navy camp had a reputation for the best food and the best hot showers—leave it to the Seabees to figure out the showers.

It is comforting to think that the millions of soldiers who passed through the camp on their way east to fight at least had a good meal and a hot shower before their ordeals ahead.

About the author

Diane Covington-Carter graduated with honors from UCLA and has received awards for her writing, photography and NPR commentaries. She has been a life coach for over thirty years, on a quest to discover the truth about the mysteries of happiness and love, both for herself and others. She lives in Northern California and New Zealand with her husband and travels to France as often as possible.

CPSIA information can be obtained at www.ICGtesting.com
Printed in the USA
LVOW04s2249301214

421011LV00014B/214/P